SIZE
TRANSITIONS
in congregations

Beth Ann Gaede, editor

Introduction by Arlin J. Rothauge

The Alban Institute

Library of Congress Card Number 00-111205
ISBN 1-56699-246-X

CONTENTS

Foreword   v

PART ONE: HOW BIG ARE WE?   1

1. Current Thinking on Size Transitions   3
   Theodore W. Johnson
2. How to Minister Effectively in Family, Pastoral, Program,
   and Corporate Sized Churches   31
   Roy M. Oswald
3. What Happens Between Sizes? Why Congregations Get Stuck   47
   Alice Mann
4. Sizing Up a Congregation: How Size Affects Function   59
   Douglas Alan Walrath
5. Leader Relationships: A Key to Congregational Size   65
   Edward II. Koster
6. Beginnings of a Theory of Synagogue Size:
   Changing Patterns and Behaviors   75
   Alice Mann, David Trietsch, and Dan Hotchkiss

PART TWO: THE UPS AND DOWNS OF CONGREGATIONAL SIZE   85

7. Growing Pains: Are They Worth It?   87
   Bill Joiner
8. Raising the Roof:
   Foundations for the Breakthrough to Program Size   93
   Alice Mann

 9. One Size Doesn't Fit All:
    Reflections on Becoming a Corporate-Size Church   119
    Joel S. McCoy
10. Marks of Growing Churches:
    The Confederate Approach to Church Growth   129
    G. W. Garvin
11. Dreaming of Cathedrals, Building Skyscrapers:
    Discovering What It Means to Be Church   135
    Elizabeth I. Steele
12. Finding Our Mission:
    Stages in the Life of an Urban Congregation   143
    Ronald T. Roberts
13. Congregations in Decline: How Context Affects Size   151
    Alice Mann
14. When Membership Declines: Letting Go and Moving Forward 155
    Roy M. Oswald
15. The Death and Dying of a Congregation:
    An Experience of God's Grace   163
    Daphne Burt

Contributors   171

During a career that has confronted me in one way or another with the challenges of understanding and developing congregations, I have been fascinated with the overwhelming influence of three variables in congregational life: context, life cycle, and size. All three factors are inherent in being alive. Size determines shape, while life cycle and context contribute continuously to the process of development. Size never exists apart from the ongoing processes at work in the life cycle and context of any given entity. It is impossible to raise questions about size without referring to the companion variables of life cycle and context.

Perhaps, however, size is the most obvious factor affecting congregational life. My identification of four convenient categories for the size of congregations initiated a starting point for discussing the development and destiny of any particular church. When we analyze a body of members in terms of any one category of this scheme for sizing up congregations, we still understand only one of the essential elements. For this reason, since I wrote *Sizing Up a Congregation for New Member Ministry* in 1983, my research and reflections have turned and expanded from the question of size to the issues of life cycle and context.

DANGEROUS CATEGORIES

If we enter the confusing realm of any particular congregation through the lens of size analysis alone, we have already distorted that mysterious reality by viewing the congregation from only one perspective. Further, categories distort the picture because they are static configurations, inadequate for objectively analyzing the dynamic processes of a vast social experience.

When we use fixed categories to examine a living organism, we start the philosophical game of defining reality by using mental constructs that reflect the complexity of reality in only a shadowy manner. Still, it is through the use of categories that we can attempt to establish an internal analogy that will help us to comprehend the external variety of existence. We must build a mental image of a world that is small enough and simple enough to be managed within the serious limitations of our human thinking. Consequently, a researcher proposes categories with certain humility.

We might presume that we have improved on the inevitable inadequacy of our categorical analysis by using more than one set of categories to guide our thinking about congregations. Nevertheless, we remind ourselves that although a fuller picture is obtained by thinking about size, context, and life cycle simultaneously, the particularity of any congregation far exceeds even that picture.

PRIMACY OF CHANGE AND SURPRISE

Should we by some miracle formulate an accurate picture of a congregation by studying several sets of key categories, we must ask ourselves, In what given moment did we mean to describe that social process? The congregation must be honored as an endless alteration of relationships and processes. In the 19th century, we all would have shared the naive assumption that establishing categories and names actually parallels and perhaps captures existence. Hence, we might have used the tools of scientific investigation to try to isolate the social laws and organizational principles that would allow us to determine the predictable shape and inevitable destiny of a congregation.

At the beginning of the 21st century, however, valid research fully acknowledges flux in form. In the postmodern period, we have fortunately moved beyond the erroneous arrogance of "scientific method."

We now approach natural and social processes expecting chaos, understanding that acts of freedom and surprising innovations must be anticipated. The presence of such creativity predisposes any complex entity toward novelty, even as a system seeks fixed patterns and normalcy. In short, we cannot know with absolute certainty the true shape and right destiny of a congregation through rational investigation and objective categories. A new shape and a more appropriate destiny may be in the making!

THE TASK OF CONGREGATIONAL STUDIES

Two decades after the publication of *Sizing Up a Congregation*, I find myself with the title professor of congregational studies. Through my role in the field, in retirement I can still contribute to doctoral students working in the academic area that has come to be known as congregational studies. I must ask myself about the purpose of this endeavor in light of the current phenomenological understanding of sociological investigation that has been briefly outlined above. Why do we still talk about the sizes of congregations? Why do we research the transition from one size to another? How can we presume to give guidance to leaders who are responsible for the course of a congregation undergoing change?

First, it is no longer our responsibility, if that mantle had been accepted mistakenly, to discover the absolute truths about congregations. There is no perfect specimen, no final formula, and no utopia—like the metaphysical and eternal forms of Plato—that guides every attempt to define congregational life. The bewildering existence of local expressions represents the reality. "Existence precedes essence."

Second, we live out the privileges of participation and leadership in a congregation by grace rather than truth. In the end the congregation is only a vehicle of a greater force of generation and innovation. We know that a congregation has fulfilled its purpose and destiny when we witness results that are determined and measured by the mission of Christianity. To be sure, in the history of our religion and in any particular century we have never found total agreement on the results that reveal the mission of God more perfectly than any others have. If we had unravelled the mystery, a new context and a new century would have changed the rules. The very diverse pilgrimage of the people of God forces us to respect surprise and contradiction as a regular aspect of being faithful to the will of God. Therefore, it is more correct, perhaps, to view each congregation more as another example of grace than truth.

Third, it seems that appreciation and anticipation best define the task of congregational studies. We know that God will work in us and through us in multiple ways. We can observe that this divine taste for variety and versatility arises from the particularity of its situation and horizons. The commitments and changes that define its process of becoming a people of God in a particular time demand its best creativity and most courageous spontaneity.

I believe that every congregation is surrounded by infinite possibilities. Choice forges a unique path through those infinite possibilities. It is the task of congregational studies to advance the appreciation of those options and enhance the anticipation of those resources in every new situation. By achieving this goal congregational research will enable leaders and members alike to acquire more skills for making wiser choices.

WE HAVE ONLY BEGUN

I am encouraged greatly when I realize that teachers, consultants, and researchers in congregational studies are pushing forward with an awareness that we have only started down the road toward an adequate understanding of the options and resources that will empower congregations to identify and work with the perplexing dynamics of their size. The pursuit of our comprehension of size and the consequences of size in a congregation's life marks an important contribution to congregational studies. We are admitting that size, perhaps the most obvious variable in congregational development, still retains many mysteries to be revealed.

THE REV. ARLIN J. ROTHAUGE, PH.D.
Founding Director of Seabury Institute
Professor of Congregational Studies
Seabury-Western Theological Seminary

PART ONE

How Big Are We?

CHAPTER 1

Current Thinking on Size Transitions

Theodore W. Johnson

When Arlin J. Rothauge published *Sizing Up a Congregation for New Member Ministry*[1] in 1983, he defined the terms mainline Protestants would use to identify congregations primarily by their sizes: family, pastoral, program, and corporation.

Rothauge's work revealed that there are four types of congregations. They differ in many ways, but the easiest difference to observe is their numerical size. The typology of congregations that Rothauge identified has since become a major feature in the lexicon of clergy and lay leaders of congregations.

ROTHAUGE'S EVANGELISTIC PURPOSE

Rothauge's purpose in writing the slim book (38 pages), published without copyright as a training document of the Episcopal Church, which employed him at the time as the national staff officer for congregational development, was unabashedly evangelistic. He wanted to know why it is that different approaches to attract and incorporate new members work in some congregations and not in others. In his research, he discovered a direct correlation between the success and failure of certain new member strategies and the size of a congregation. As he stated in the introduction: "The most effective means of carrying out a new member ministry varies with the size of the congregation."[2]

Thus, a *family* church incorporates new members the way a *family* does—by birth, marriage, and adoption. A *pastoral* church does it based almost exclusively on the relationship the newcomers develop with the *pastor*. New members of a *program* church are primarily attracted by the congregation's *programs*, whether for children or adults, whether for music, study, service, support, education, or fellowship. And a *corporation* church draws newcomers with its human, financial, and physical resources for high quality ministries that rival major secular *corporations* and that operate in a fashion similar to them.

From one perspective, given Rothauge's intention to encourage church leaders to undertake aggressive evangelistic approaches that appropriately matched their type, *Sizing Up a Congregation for New Member Ministry* was a failure. For example, family-sized churches, seeking to enlarge their dwindling membership rolls, continued to undertake newcomer activities appropriate to program churches and then wondered why their membership remained stagnant.

Nevertheless, Rothauge's book had a revolutionary impact on congregations and their leaders because it described four different ways of being a congregation, four different congregational cultures. People read the book and ignored the evangelistic intent. (Should we in mainline denominations be surprised?) Still, the book describes realities of congregational life that no one had previously identified.

A sociological axiom underlying these new realities is that the size of an aggregate determines its organization. Thus, each of the four types of congregations has its own unique organization defined primarily by its leadership structure and relationship style. Leadership structure describes the way a congregation governs its life, particularly the roles and functions of its key leaders. Relationship style describes the way the members of the congregation relate to one another.

Until Rothauge defined the four types of congregations, the operating assumption for most congregational leaders was that all congregations functioned in basically the same way. As Rothauge put it in his introduction: "The purpose of this presentation is to demonstrate how one important factor, the size of congregations, prevents us from using one program and one style of leadership for all church situations."[3] Yet, examples abound of clergy seeking to implement in their congregations ideas, ministries, policies, and strategies that worked in a congregation of a different size. Not surprisingly, these clergy experience a level of failure, rejection, and frustration that shapes their future as ordained leaders, often negatively.

"AHA!" MOMENTS

Immediately after seminary, I was called to serve as the assistant to the rector of a pastoral church that aspired to become a program church. That is, key lay leaders wanted an assistant to the rector who would design and implement programs for youth and adult education that were typical of a program church—but that are as rare in a pastoral-size church as an assistant to the rector. The rector, nearing retirement, had no desire for such programs and expected the assistant to lighten his existing workload, not add to it.

For reasons I did not understand at the time, my ministry in the congregation was a disaster in the making and lasted less than a year from my hiring to my firing. The existing leadership structure and relationship style of the congregation did not require an assistant to the rector. Nor did the current organizational dynamics match the programs that a few leaders in the congregation desired. No doubt the leaders saw such programs in nearby larger churches and believed that all congregations should have them.

When I read Rothauge's book in the emotional and spiritual aftermath of this experience, the proverbial light bulb went on and I had that "Aha!" moment of recognition. My call to that position was based on a mistaken attempt to implement the activities appropriate to one type of congregation in a congregation of a very different type.

My next assignment was to be the rector of a family church that had grown in size to about 85 people in "average Sunday attendance." Having read Rothauge, this term had become part of my thinking about congregations—family: 1 to 50; pastoral: 51 to 150; program: 151 to 350; corporation: 351 and up. (These are Rothauge's original numbers, some of which, as I will discuss later, may need reconsideration.)

Based on the average Sunday attendance, I believed that I was serving a pastoral church that might, because of population growth in the area, became a program church. Two years and much anguish later, I came to realize as I left the congregation that it was in fact a family church with an enlarged average Sunday attendance resulting from several unique factors. My total focus on the average Sunday attendance blinded me to the true nature of the leadership structure (dominated by matriarchs and patriarchs) and the relationship style (extended families and clans). I was trying to be the pastor at the hub of the wheel (typical for a pastoral church) in a congregation that regarded its clergy as largely irrelevant chaplains whose job was—typical of a family church—only to preach, lead worship, care for the sick, open meetings with a prayer, and not get in the way of the matriarchs and patriarchs who ran the business of the congregation.

In the midst of this experience, I read Rothauge's book again and had the opportunity to hear him present his theories. Too late to salvage my ministry in that congregation, I realized that I had, along with two immediate predecessors, misinterpreted the situation. The family-church culture was dominant. Again, I experienced an "Aha!" moment.

My experience since then has been that clergy and lay leaders have those same "Aha!" moments when they learn that there are four types of congregations that are very different from each other. As I present the typology to groups of leaders in varieties of settings, I hear that clear laughter of recognition as they see which type of congregation theirs really is, despite their desires or expectations that the situation be otherwise.

Although Rothauge's original evangelistic intent did not take hold, the descriptions of the four types or cultures of congregations constitute the enduring contribution of *Sizing Up a Congregation for New Member Ministry*. The book accurately described the reality of congregational life in the four very different forms it takes.

MAKING ROOM FOR NEW MEMBERS

Rothauge's book did have evangelistic consequences, however, although they were different from what he intended. Instead of educating leaders about how to appropriately attract and incorporate new members into the four types of congregations, the book demonstrated the need for congregations to grow in order to make room for new members. Countless churches are located in areas of increasing population and almost every Sunday attract church-shopping visitors who never return. The reason: these churches have no room—physically, emotionally, or numerically—for additional members.

Lack of physical room is fairly easy to see—insufficient seating in the worship space, too few spaces in the parking lot, not enough or not large enough rooms for Sunday school and fellowship. The remedy may be either to expand the facilities or to increase the number of worship services and other program offerings.

Less obvious is the lack of emotional room for new members. For example, pastoral churches tend to attract new members who desire the leadership structure and relationship style of a pastoral church; visitors seeking a different type will continue their church shopping until they find a church of their preferred type. The reasons for the preference are subtle, not often clearly stated—as are the reasons some people prefer to shop in large, enclosed malls with parking lots or garages, and others prefer strip shopping centers where they can park directly in front of the store where they will shop.

The clues to these emotional preferences appear in statements like the following: "I like the family feel of this congregation." (The person is looking for a family congregation.) "I'm looking for a congregation where the pastor really knows me." (Here is someone looking for a pastoral congregation.) "The other congregations we visited were too big and impersonal for my comfort level; this is just right for me to get to know everyone." (This person's preference is for a family or pastoral congregation.) "We are especially interested in finding interesting activities for our children." (These people would probably need a program congregation.) "I want a high quality worship experience, with inspiring, dynamic preaching by a highly charismatic senior pastor, concert-hall quality music, and a wide variety of well-run activities where I can find my own place." (Nothing but a corporation congregation will work for this visitor.) "The other congregations were too small and personal for my comfort level; this is just right for me to be anonymous." (A program or corporation congregation is most likely to satisfy this person.)

Of course, what I am discussing as a lack of emotional room for new members is really a mismatch between the congregation's current type and the preferences of church-shopping visitors. However, as neighborhoods change, the possibility increasingly exists that the majority of potential new members in the area will prefer a congregation of a type different from the churches already in the neighborhood. Making emotional room for new members might require a transition from the current type to that preferred by the people in the neighborhood, especially if many of the people would need to travel some distance to find a church that matched their preference.

Still less obvious is the lack of room for new members created because a congregation has reached the maximum size for its type, even though there may be plenty of physical room for substantial growth. If such a congregation wishes to maintain the leadership structure and relationship style of its current type, the congregation cannot incorporate many more new members. Congregations tend to plateau near these maximum sizes, and all efforts to attract new members—even those who may value the congregation's current type—fail, because there is no numerical room for them.

Whether church leaders face a plateau in membership or most potential members in the neighborhood prefer a different type of congregation, Rothauge's book helps them recognize that the real issue is not simply attracting and incorporating new members, but first, and more importantly, making room for them. The task is not one of congregational growth, but of transition in size from one type of congregation to another. A transition in size is required not only to provide the emotional and numerical room for an increase in membership, but also to adapt to a sharp decrease in the number of members in a congregation. Whatever the nature of the transition, the main task is to change the relationship style and leadership structure to those appropriate to the type of congregation that will emerge from the transition.

Making such a transition is no small task, and it differs greatly from what most leaders consider when they attempt congregational growth. Trained greeters, advertising, mailings, seeker-friendly worship, new and different worship services, follow-up visits and mailings, attractive signage, and the like are all valuable techniques for church growth. But they fail miserably when there is no emotional or numerical room in the congregation for new members. Many congregations have attempted a transition in type, often from pastoral to program, using church growth techniques and have become frustrated with their lack of success because the transition in size required changing the very culture of the congregation, the essence of what makes it attractive to current members.

THE REAL ISSUE: SIZE TRANSITION

Soon after publishing *Sizing Up a Congregation for New Member Ministry*, Rothauge realized that making room for new members was the key evangelistic task facing the church. Indeed, my conversations with Rothauge have revealed that he sees transitions in general as the primary focus of congregational development, with the transition in size as the most crucial for the future of the church.

This emphasis on transitions is reflected in Rothauge's publications that followed *Sizing Up a Congregation for New Member Ministry*.

The first, *A Church Is Born: Basics for Starting and Developing a Mission Congregation*,[4] written in 1984, discussed the planting of a new congregation and its likely transitions in size as it grew from family to pastoral, from pastoral to program, and, possibly from program to corporation. This approach has since been displaced by strategies developed at the Charles E. Fuller Institute of Evangelism and Church Growth and elsewhere. These strategies begin with the premise that a new congregation should be established as a program congregation, so it will not have to go through the difficult transitions that have often limited the growth of new congregations that started out as family or pastoral churches.

Then came *Reshaping a Congregation for a New Future* (about 1985),[5] which discussed the nature of transitions in general and detailed transitions in three circumstances—size, life cycle, and community context. In this book, Rothauge presented for the first time his theory about the life cycle of a congregation, which he wrote about again in 1993 in *The Life Cycle in Congregations: A Process of Natural Creation and an Opportunity for New Creation*.[6] Although Rothauge is not the only writer to develop a congregational life cycle theory, he identified three useful strategies for congregational transitions—redefinition, redevelopment, and rebirth, which differ in the length of time and intensity of change required. (I call them "resurrection pathways" in my presentations.) Although not as well known as Rothauge's theory of congregational size, I view the life cycle theory of equal importance for congregational development. *Parallel Development: A Pathway for Exploring Change and a New Future in Congregational Life* (about 1987),[7] followed, presenting a strategy for transitions that places two different ways of being a church—one previously existing and the other newly initiated—side-by-side. Then came *Making Small Groups Effective: Notes on Fellowships, Home Cell Groups, and House Churches in the Episcopal Tradition* (about 1993),[8] an introduction for establishing small groups in a congregation. Finally *All Doors Open: Congregational Strategies for Comprehensive Evangelism and Outreach* (about 1994)[9] described three primary ways for new members to enter a congregation. All of these works subsequent to *Sizing Up a Congregation for New Member Ministry* addressed various aspects of congregational transitions and are especially useful for transitions in size. As with *Sizing Up a Congregation for New Member Ministry*, all the books were published by the Episcopal Church and were not covered by copyright. Five of them, *Sizing Up, Life Cycle, Parallel Development, Small*

Groups, and *All Doors Open*, are part of The Congregational Vitality Series.

ROTHAUGE'S THEORY MISUNDERSTOOD AND MISAPPLIED

Although the main strength of the Rothauge theory has been its "Aha!"-producing descriptions of the four congregational cultures, many leaders have misunderstood and misapplied the theory. I have identified four typical misunderstandings.

Just Labels for Sunday Attendance

Some people misunderstand the four types as mere labels for broad ranges of average Sunday attendance. This misunderstanding ignores the fact that the four types describe different cultures with their own unique relationship style and leadership structure. Average worship attendance is not the only variable among the four types. Many congregation leaders have been misled, as I was in the second congregation I served, when the worship attendance fits one type and the relationship style and leadership structure fit another type.

It is not unusual for this discrepancy to occur. Such apparent exceptions to the size theory abound and are often easy to understand once one recognizes that the three primary variables of attendance, relationship style, and leadership structure are all dynamic. More often than not, the relationship style and the leadership structure—not attendance—will accurately indicate the actual type of the congregation.

The Numbers Game

Some people misunderstand the theory and dismiss it as irrelevant to the true purposes of congregation life. "We don't play 'the numbers game' in this congregation," they say. "Instead, we emphasize the quality of our ministries and their effects on people's lives—spiritual growth—not whether we are meeting some arbitrary numerical target set by a bureaucrat at national church headquarters."

I believe that Sunday worship attendance figures are important measurements of congregational health and movement that we ignore at our peril. I find it interesting that the biblical witness in the Acts of the Apostles is clear that the early church placed great importance on membership figures. However, people who hold "the numbers game" misunderstanding seem to recognize correctly that the other variables of leadership structure and relationship style are in fact more important than the variable of size in determining the culture of a congregation.

The Ladder of Success

Some church leaders regard the two larger types as successful and the two smaller as failures. This attitude often appears among clergy seeking a yardstick by which to measure their careers. In Episcopal circles the unstated aspiration is, "If I can't be a bishop, at least I want to retire from a program or corporation church." Other clergy seem to be embarrassed by the type of congregation they currently serve, saying, "I serve a family congregation now, but I'm in a search to move to a program church." Or they comment, "I serve a pastoral church, but it is on the way to becoming program." Lay leaders, when comparing their congregation to others in their community or in their judicatory, will say, "We're *just* a pastoral (or family) church."

The underlying low self-esteem associated with being clergy and members of family or pastoral congregations is unfortunate and clearly neither explicit nor implicit in Rothauge's theory. In fact, he clearly stated, "There is no intent in this presentation to attach any stigma or respectability to size as such. On the contrary, it is assumed that any size church is the right size, and any size church can attract and assimilate new members."[10]

Although the larger congregations account for a greater proportion of total membership in the United States, the majority of congregations in most denominations today are family or pastoral types. It is not realistic to think that all these congregations and their clergy must or can move up some imaginary ladder of success.

In my work as a consultant with congregations, I seek to affirm pastoral and family congregations and encourage leaders to find ways for the congregations to be as vital and effective as possible in today's changing climate. There are, however, very real pressures on smaller congregations today.

One pressure is the increasing cost of clergy compensation (including salary, housing allowance, health insurance premiums, and pension contributions) and basic congregational operating expenses. Another pressure is a deepening shortage of clergy and in particular of clergy who feel called to serve smaller congregations. For example, a group of deployment officers from certain dioceses in the Episcopal Church meets twice a year to share the names of congregations searching for clergy and of clergy searching for new assignments. At the group's meeting in March 2001, there were six congregations looking for clergy for every clergy person seeking a new assignment. Further, the majority of the congregations were family and pastoral types, and the majority of clergy preferred to serve program and corporation congregations, whether as senior pastor or as an associate.

A third pressure today is rising societal expectations for the quality of facilities, staff, and ministries. These expectations make it difficult for smaller congregations to compete for members with larger congregations that have greater resources, improved economies of scale, and more participants in activities. Young members of small churches often express the desire to attend a larger congregation where there is a youth leader on staff, where the youth group does "lots of interesting things," and where "I will not be the only eighth grader in the youth group."

I believe that God's Spirit is at work in the midst of these pressures, calling some pastoral congregations to undertake the transition to program size—not to climb a ladder of success, not to raise congregational self-esteem, not to ensure survival in a new environment—but to make room for unchurched people who are hungry for the life-transforming power of God experienced through the body of Christ.

Nevertheless, not every congregation is called to make a transition to a larger type. Every congregation must be clear about its identity, expressed in terms of (1) God's call to a specific mission or purpose and (2) God's promise of a specific future or vision. If God's call and promise are best lived out as a family or pastoral church, then a congregation should find ways through increased financial support from its members or through new models for deployment of clergy to be faithful to that call and promise.

But We're Different

The protest "But we're different" occurs when congregations are basically satisfied with their current size, but some leaders are unwilling to accept the descriptions of the relationship style or the leadership structure that go with it. Like "the ladder of success," this misunderstanding is also linked to levels of self-esteem and to the perception that certain roles are negative or positive. It surfaces in family churches, for example, when the recognized lay leaders that everyone looks to for direction refuse to accept that they are functioning as matriarchs or patriarchs. "But we're different," they say. The clergy in the same congregations may be unable to accept their actual status as chaplains and repeat the same refrain. In pastoral churches, the clergy may not wish to see themselves as the master coordinators of all aspects of parish life with the autocratic control this frequently gives them. "But we're different," they say, along with the members of the central governing body of the same congregations who do not wish to accept their role as designated task-doers and deny that they micromanage all issues that come before them.

What the people who hold these four misunderstandings of the Rothauge theory have in common is the inability to see the types as unique cultures with only three principal variables. Those with the fourth misunderstanding dismiss the theory because they are personally uncomfortable with one or more of its descriptions of their role or functioning. But leaders who harbor the other three misunderstandings focus on size to the exclusion of the other two variables, relationship style and leadership structure. Such overemphasis on numerical size and neglect of the other variables has resulted not only in misunderstanding the theory, but also in misapplying it to congregations.

THE CONGRUENCE THEORY

When I worked on a doctor of ministry in the congregational development program at Seabury-Western Theological Seminary—a program that Arlin Rothauge founded after he left the staff of the Episcopal Church—I was serving as the interim pastor for a congregation that had the average Sunday attendance of a large pastoral church (about 150). But it had a family church's leadership structure (matriarchs and patriarchs with a clergy chaplain) and relationship style (a few clans not connected by familial ties but by common interests and circumstances).

I titled a study of this congregation that I submitted to Rothauge "The Largest Family-Sized Church in the World." Although clearly an exaggeration, the title spoke a truth about apparent exceptions to the Rothauge theory. It is possible for the size of a congregation to be mismatched with the other variables that determine a congregation's type. In this case, roughly 100 people worshipped with this congregation on Sunday but were not involved in any other aspects of congregational life. I called them "worship-only" members; they did not participate in the fellowship, education, community service, or other ministries. They did not pledge or share in any leadership responsibilities. They were essentially inactive members except for worship. Financial support, leadership, education, fellowship, and all other ministries depended on a group of about 50 members. The congregation was actually a family church with an extraordinarily large Sunday attendance.

With encouragement from Rothauge, I devoted my doctoral thesis[11] to accounting for apparent exceptions to his theory and developed a companion theory called "congruence in congregational size." This theory holds that the principal variables that determine a congregation's type must be congruent with one another for that congregation to function effectively in its type. The congregation I served was dysfunctional because fully two-thirds of its worshiping members were not in relationship with each other or with the other third. They were not able to participate as members of the body of Christ manifest in that congregation.

The chart that follows shows that not only the numerical attendance, but also the relationship style and the leadership structure are unique to each type of congregation. Thus, the relationship style of a family church is not duplicated in any of the other three types, nor is the leadership structure of a program church. Each type has its own distinct way of being a congregation, and that distinctiveness is seen in each variable.

Type	Size	Relationship Style	Leadership Structure
Family	1-50	One group consists of tightly knit extended families or "clans" that center on matriarchs and patriarchs.	Family matriarchs and patriarchs make decisions. Pastor (part time, retired?) functions as chaplain. Board conducts business and ministries in support of matriarchs and patriarchs. Other staff—usually a musician—is part-time and performs a limited but essential function.
Pastoral	51-150	One large group centers on the pastor, with some members in loosely knit functional or friendship circles.	Pastor is the hub of the wheel, master coordinator, chief minister. Board members are short-term task-doers, micro-decision makers. Ministry coordinators are permanent task-doers who value close working relationship with the pastor. Other staff—usually a musician and a secretary—is part-time and performs limited but essential functions.
Program	151-350	Two or more distinct worshiping congregations include one-third of all members (in small groups of 5 to 15 people) that center on skilled and empowered staff or lay leaders.	Program groups/teams/committees have their own empowered lay leaders and plan and implement programs and activities. Board members are managers, policy-makers who oversee but do not lead program groups/teams/committees. Pastor functions as the executive. Other staff (one or more ordained) includes full- and part-time assistants to pastor, program resources.
Corporation	351+	More than two worshiping congregations include half of all members coalescing by affinity into small "congregations" of 30+ people.	Pastor is chief executive officer, with mythic qualities. Staff (several ordained) includes full-time executives in charge of program areas. Program groups/teams/committees with virtual autonomy operate programs as almost independent organizations. Board functions as board of directors.

Vertical band labels (left to right):
- Size scale: SMALL — MEDIUM — LARGE
- Relationship Style: CELL — SINGLE CELL — MULTIPLE CELL — MULTIPLE
- Leadership Structure: INDIVIDUAL — INDIVIDUAL — COLLABORATOR — COLLABORATOR

Four Dimensions of the Congruence Theory

The theory of congruence in congregational size adds three new dimensions to the descriptive dimension that was present in the original Rothauge theory. These are the diagnostic, prescriptive, and transforming dimensions. The descriptive dimension (in Rothauge's theory) describes the realities of the four different types of congregations.

The diagnostic dimension helps leaders and outside observers, such as judicatory officials or consultants, identify potential areas of dysfunction in a congregation when one variable is not congruent with the others. In the example of the largest family-sized congregation in the world, the diagnostic dimension identified that the variable of numerical size was not congruent with the variables of leadership structure and relationship style.

The prescriptive dimension helps leaders and observers to reduce dysfunction and bring health and effectiveness to a congregation by obtaining congruence among the three variables. In the example of the largest family-sized congregation in the world, the prescriptive dimension discredited the goal of some lay leaders that the next installed pastor would move the congregation from a pastoral to a program church, a goal that was popular among search committees in the area at the time. The leaders' operating assumption, based only on Sunday worship attendance, was that the congregation was on the verge of becoming a program church. Instead of this unrealistic goal, the prescriptive dimension could suggest that the congregation accept the current situation, embracing the leadership structure and relationship style of a family church with an extraordinarily large number of worship-only members. This decision would produce an uneasy and perhaps undesirable congruence as a family church but would preclude initiating unrealistic building programs and other goals for major growth.

The transforming dimension helps leaders and observers move the congregation from one type to another. In my example, the transforming dimension would identify the specific changes that need to be made for the congregation to change its relationship style and leadership structure from those of a family church to those of a pastoral church, thereby opening room in the congregation to more fully incorporate the worship-only members as participants in all areas of congregational life. Such a transition would bring congruence among the actual attendance, relationship style, and leadership structure of a healthy pastoral church. I stress that this congregation would not have the room to incorporate fully the worship-only members unless it changed its relationship style and leadership structure.

The Building Blocks of Congregations

A strategic framework for transitions from one congregational type to another has been lacking. The congruence theory complemented the original Rothauge theory by providing more detailed descriptions of the leadership structure and relationship style of a congregation before and after a transition and made clear the overall goal of bringing them into congruence with the numerical size. What was still needed was a clear, simple road map for moving from one type to another. As I have noted earlier, even the best church growth techniques are not adequate for a transition that changes the culture of a congregation.

Information about group size, based on anthropological research, was crucial in designing the necessary road map. Rothauge discovered this information in the book *The Tipping Point: How Little Things Can Make a Big Difference* by Malcolm Gladwell.[12] He shared the information with me, and I used it to define three basic building blocks that are used to construct all congregations. These building blocks (see following page) provide the road map for a transition from one type of congregation to another.

Family and pastoral congregations, consisting of a single cell, each use only one building block. Program and corporation congregations, consisting of multiple cells, use all three building blocks in various configurations.

The smallest building block is the small group with 12 to 15 people. It is in these settings that relationships of the greatest intimacy and mutual care and support occur. Anthropologists call the small group a "sympathy group,"[13] based on the fact that most people, when asked to list the people for whom they will profoundly grieve when they die, list about 12 family members and friends, and rarely does the list exceed 15.

We almost never see a true small group in family or pastoral congregations. But it is an important building block for program and corporation churches. In such churches the small groups consist of people who gather for study or prayer, for mutual support (single parents, bereaved, or recently divorced people), and the like. Generally, a small group in a congregation has some degree of homogeneity, perhaps in age, educational level resources, or circumstances. It has its own leader, who serves as both convener of the group's meetings and its connecting agent or shepherd between meetings.

The next building block is the primary group, which is larger than the small group but has no more than 50 people. I use this term to describe an intergenerational group that functions like a family. Its leadership

Building Blocks of Congregations

Small Group/
Sympathy Group
No more than 15 people

Primary Group/
Famly Group
No more than 50 people

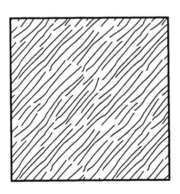

Community Group/
Village Group/
Fellowship Group
No more than 150 people

is entrusted to respected elders. Members receive rights and privileges based on their age, relationship to the elders, family position, and often gender. The primary group may actually be an extended family or clan whose members are related by birth and marriage. Or it may be like a tribe with more than one extended family. Or it may be a group of unrelated people formed by a common circumstance that continues over a period of time and in which a family-like style of governance emerges.

Family Church
A stand-alone family group
(single cell)

The family church is a stand-alone primary group. When referring to churches, I prefer to use the term "family group," because it defines more accurately the essential dynamic of this size group in congregational settings. Pastoral churches usually do not have family groups, but family groups are crucial building blocks for both program and corporation congregations. The early worship service in some congregations is often a family group, as is the choir, the corps of Sunday school teachers, the youth group, the Sunday morning Bible class, and the like. A family group in a congregation is to some extent heterogeneous, combining people of differing ages, educational levels, resources, and circumstances who are united by a common purpose or activity.

The governance of family groups in congregations is family-style, with the most respected people serving as leaders (the choir director, the Sunday school superintendent, the youth group advisor). Members' roles, rights, and privileges are determined by respect and position.

The third building block is the community group, which is larger than the primary group but has no more than 150 members. Anthropologist Robin Dunbar[14] has determined that this is the largest possible group in which human beings can be in active relationship with each other. Dunbar believes that in primates, the number of relationships an individual can manage is primarily the consequence of neocortex size. The neocortex portion of the human brain, although significantly larger than that of other primates, is only large enough to handle the complexities of active relationships in a group of no more than 150 people. Other primates cannot come close to managing this many relationships, however.

According to Dunbar, the human brain is large enough to contain the knowledge not only of an individual's active relationships with all the other members of the community group, but also of the active relationships that all the members of the group have with each other. In a group of four, each member would have knowledge of six active relationships (A with B, A with C, A with D, B with C, B with D, and C with D). As the group size increases, the number of active relationships in the group increases exponentially. For example if the group is five times larger and includes 20 people, each member would have knowledge of 190 active relationships, a number roughly 32 times larger than in a group of four. When our brains try to manage the largest group we can deal with, about 150 people, most of the members of the group need a facilitator who can help them maintain knowledge of that many active relationships. Community groups can be of any size between 50 and 150, with the most comfortable being around 100, which we might call the ideal community group.

The community group is sometimes called a village group, because it corresponds to typical village sizes in a variety of eras, locations, and cultures. It appears that human beings are naturally aware of this upper limit in relationship capacity and have organized their lives accordingly. The community group is governed by a council, whose members serve with the legitimate or coerced consent of the group itself. The principal leader may maintain the position by popularity, acknowledged skill or experience, charisma, personal respect, or force.

Pastoral Church
A stand-alone fellowship group
(single cell)

The pastoral church is a stand-alone community group. When referring to congregations, I prefer to use the term "fellowship group" to avoid confusion with groups in the neighborhood or larger community. "Fellowship group" also captures the essence of the functioning of this size group in congregational settings. The pastor facilitates the relationships of the group members, making it easy for them to be in active relationship with the others, even if they do not have complete knowledge of all the active relationships in the group.

Obviously, the fellowship group cannot exist in the smaller family church, but it is a building block for program and corporation churches. In many cases, those attending the principal worship services in program and corporation churches are members of fellowship groups, having active relationships with their own worshipping congregation but not with all those at other worship services. Remember that program and corporation churches have multiple cells (building blocks) that exist alongside but are not fully merged with each other. I find it interesting that many program churches have less than 150 in attendance at each of their several worship services.

Another fellowship group in program and corporation congregations includes the children and teachers in the Sunday school.

Program Church
An amalgam of small, family, and fellowship groups
(Multiple cells)

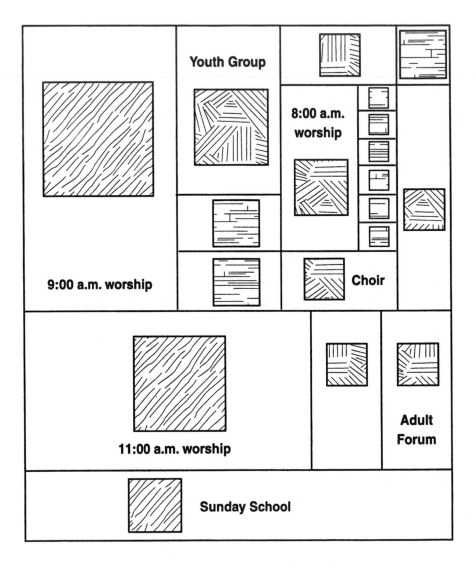

Generally, a program church–depending on its overall size–may consist of 10 to 20 small groups, fewer than 10 family groups, and only two or three fellowship groups.

Corporate Church
A much larger amalgam of small, family, and fellowship groups
(Multiple cells)

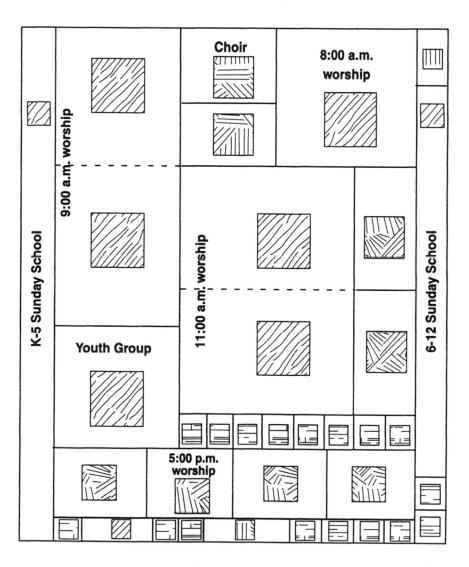

A corporation church has more of each type of building block. The fellowship groups and family groups in corporation churches have high levels of autonomy to manage their affairs, possessing many characteristics of completely independent mini-congregations within the larger umbrella of the corporation church. Each of the main worship services in a corporation church may actually be subdivided into two or more fellowship groups whose identities are shaped by activities other than worshipping together, such as fellowship or education. Further, a significant number of worshippers are not in active relationships with other members of the congregation, preferring to remain relatively anonymous. Unique to a corporation church is a fellowship group that has total responsibility for a major activity, such as Lenten preaching services with sit-down lunches served before and after, or the operation of a hospital, school, or other institution in a Third World country.

It is easy for us to understand the family church as a stand-alone family group and the pastoral church as a stand-alone fellowship group. In single cells, almost all the members are in active relationship with each other. The relationship style and the leadership structure of the family church and pastoral church are different, but in both cases the simplicity of the single cell is appreciated and cherished by the members.

On the other hand, the program church and the corporation church, consisting of multiple cells, are highly complex. The building blocks—small groups, family groups, and fellowship groups—are assembled in a variety of configurations with no set pattern, in differing sizes within their ranges, and with varying connections or lack of connections with each other. It is probably true that no two program or corporation churches assemble the building blocks in quite the same way.

THE BUILDING BLOCKS AND TRANSITIONS IN SIZE

Identifying the building blocks that are used to construct congregations raises issues and highlights ramifications that affect clergy and lay leaders in each type of congregation. This chapter is not the vehicle to discuss them. It must be noted, however, that any strategy for transition from one size to another must take into account the building blocks I have described. A transition in size is not just a matter of increasing membership or starting a new and different worship service, but of changing the culture of the congregation. When a family church seeks to make the transition to a pastoral church, it must give up functioning as a family group and become a fellowship group. When a pastoral church seeks to accomplish the transition to a program church, it must give up being a single cell in which almost every member is in active relationship with each other and become a multiple cell in which the members are distributed among the building blocks of small groups, family groups, and fellowship groups in a complex configuration. When a program church seeks to become a corporation church, it must take on a far greater degree of complexity as members of each mini-congregation have greater autonomy and independence from each other.

The proportion of worship-only members increases as the numerical size of the congregation increases. Greater complexity allows for greater anonymity. It is easier to hide in a complex organization than in a simple one, which means that larger congregations may have more members, without a corresponding increase in active participation.

Once church leaders see the four types of congregations in terms of their building blocks, they should not be surprised that attempted transitions in congregational size fail more often than they succeed. In particular, they can understand why the transition from a pastoral congregation to a program congregation, which may be the most appropriate response to pressures facing churches today, is often resisted by clergy, lay leaders, and members who prefer the simplicity of the single cell to the complexity of multiple cells, and who prefer being in a congregation that consists of only one, not many, building blocks.

Two Ways to Grow

The writers of some of the chapters in this volume suggest strategies for making a transition in congregational size. Although this guidance is helpful, the reader should not be misled into thinking that such transitions are easy. Most, but not all, transitions in congregational size involve numerical growth of the congregation. I have stressed, however, that such transitions require more than basic church growth techniques, because when a congregation makes a transition in size, it must change the culture of the congregation, often contrary to the preference of many existing members who are satisfied with the current relationship style and leadership structure. Size transitions are far more complicated than many believe and are often filled with pain, resistance, outright sabotage, and inevitable membership disruption.

Leaders of pastoral congregations must keep the congregational build-ing blocks in mind as a strategic road map for the transition to a program church, bringing into existence several new building blocks—small groups, family groups, and fellowship groups—alongside the existing single fellow-ship group. Similarly, leaders of family churches must guide their congrega-tion through an evolution from a family group to a fellowship group in the transition to a pastoral church. And leaders of a program church will bring into existence new building blocks and increase the size of current ones as they achieve a transition to a corporation church.

It is helpful also to remember that congregations grow in two different ways: incrementally and transitionally. *Incremental growth* in a congrega-tion will increase the number of members in a congregation incrementally but will not accomplish a transition from one type to another. For example, a pastoral church can move from 100 to 145 Sunday worshipers, but it will still be a pastoral church and will most likely plateau at that level. Basic church growth techniques produce incremental growth.

Mention church growth to most church leaders and they think of incre-mental growth—expanding the congregation gradually over time until it reaches some expected goal in the future. Most often the approach works well at the beginning as new members are added but then bumps into a ceiling, the upper limit for the congregation's current type. Expansion stops at that point, and leaders experience disappointment and frustration, espe-cially if their goal was to move through a transition from one type to an-other.

Transitional growth in a congregation will not only increase the num-ber of members in a congregation, but will also accomplish the transition from one type to another. A congregation accomplishes transitional growth by adding new building blocks—small groups, family groups, and fellowship groups—alongside the existing ones, which also may grow incrementally (up to their maximum size limits) at the same time. The new building blocks create room for the congregation to grow from one type to another.

Many congregational leaders balk at working toward transitional growth. Compared to the amount of effort and degree of change required to achieve incremental growth, transitional growth is indeed a frightening prospect. If God's call and promise for a congregation include a transition from one congregational type to another, however, transitional growth is the only real-istic and effective option.

DEFICIENCIES OF THE ROTHAUGE THEORY

The Rothauge theory of congregational size is not yet finished. I have shown how the companion theory of congruence in congregational size and the empirically determined understanding of sizes in social groups augment Rothauge's theory in significant ways. More work is needed, however.

Many leaders and members of congregations complain about the terms "family," "pastoral," "program," and "corporation." As I noted earlier in this essay, Rothauge chose logical terms that were appropriate to his original purpose of correlating congregational size and new member ministries. Some congregational developers have substituted "matriarchal/patriarchal" for "family." Not surprisingly, many in pastoral churches object to the "program" term as cold and impersonal. No one to my knowledge has suggested more accurate or memorable alternatives, however. Perhaps the most vulnerable term is "corporation," which is probably too secular sounding to be used as a label for a congregation. The type name has in practice evolved from "corporation," which Rothauge originally used, to "corporate," which most leaders use. One alternative that has gained some currency is "resource," which captures some of the essence of what makes this type of congregation distinctive. Personally, I have no pressing need to change the terms, but I could easily accept "resource" instead of "corporation."

A far more significant deficiency in the typology is the upper size of the program church. Rothauge put it at 350 in average Sunday attendance. He and I have discussed this on various occasions and agree that 350 is probably too low. New research on program churches is needed, especially in light of the building blocks of congregations, to gain a better knowledge of how these building blocks are assembled and connected with each other. I predict that the new research will show that the leadership structure and the relationship style of the program church exist when the average Sunday attendance approaches 1000, with an "ideal size" for the program church at about 450.

New research is also needed about the corporation church. Looking at a corporation church in terms of its building blocks invites further study of how they are configured and connected.

Another unexamined issue involves churches that operate preschools, day-care centers, or elementary and high schools. Are the students and their parents part of the congregational culture even though they do not worship with the congregation? Clearly, the congregation is providing a ministry to these families. But does a school with 100 students sponsored by a congregation with 125 worshipping members affect the leadership structure and the relationship style of that congregation in such a way that it is a program church, not a pastoral one?

Still another crucial issue is the size distinction between the corporation church and the so-called megachurch or metachurch, a phenomenon that has come into existence since Rothauge published the size theory. Although megachurches are rare in mainline denominations, they are a reality in church life today, and any theory of congregational size must take them into account. New research is needed not only to determine the minimum size of the megachurch, which will also be the upper limit of a corporation church, but also to define its unique leadership structure and relationship style. In other words, there is probably now in existence a fifth type of congregation, which has not been accurately described.

Some congregational developers have suggested there may be still another distinct type of congregation, the so-called transitional church or in-between church. In practice these terms have been applied to any congregation with an average Sunday attendance between 150 and 250, whether or not the congregation is intentionally or actually making the transition from pastoral to program. Rothauge and I do not view these congregations as a distinct type, but the term may be an appropriate label for the temporary phase congregations experience as they make the transition from one type of church to another. During this transitional phase, the congregations are no longer true examples of the type they were and not yet true examples of the type they are becoming. This phase occurs in all size transitions, not just the one from pastoral to program.

In my experience, a surprising number of congregations that have between 150 and 250 in average Sunday attendance are actually pastoral churches with the leadership structure and relationship style of a pastoral church, but with an exceptionally large Sunday attendance. The exceptional Sunday attendance often occurs in pastoral churches that have enjoyed the leadership of extremely capable pastoral church clergy who have had an unusually long and positive tenure with the congregation. Such gifted clergy are able to facilitate the active relationships of well over 150 people while maintaining them in the single cell of a fellowship group. When those pastors leave, the congregations frequently shrink to the worship attendance that is typical of pastoral churches.

However, some congregations in this size range of 150 to 250 worshippers are making the transition from a pastoral to a program church.

When we study them more closely, I believe we will discover that parallel to the leadership structure and relationship style of a pastoral church are now emerging the leadership structure and relationship style of a program church. In addition, we will see that the single cell of a stand-alone fellowship group is being transformed into a multiple-cell configuration of small group, family group, and fellowship group building blocks. Further, we will see both incremental growth and transitional growth. This pattern would apply for all transitions in congregational size.

CONCLUSION

For the past 15 years, I have been fascinated with the way the Rothauge theory of congregational size has described the reality of congregational life. One of the discussions that Rothauge and I have had on more than one occasion concerns identifying the single most definitive element in each of the four types. Our current conclusion is that matriarchs and patriarchs are the central feature of the family church. The pastor's role as the master coordinator of all ministries is the chief mark of the pastoral church. Empowered lay leaders who function as shepherds for small, family, and fellowship groups define the program church. Multiple mini-congregations of various sizes are the key feature of the corporation church.

When a family church has a summer picnic, the different extended families or clans each take separate tables and share food that they brought only for that particular group. When a pastoral church has a picnic, all the food is placed on a central table, and all members take from it what they wish and then find seats at tables in totally random fashion with no preference about table companions. When a program church has a picnic, the members of the different groups in the congregation—Bible study, choir, Sunday school teachers, and the like—sit as groups and share only the food that they brought for that group. Corporation churches do not have picnics, but the mini-congregations of the corporation churches do. The gatherings will be similar to the picnics of the family church, the pastoral church, or program church, depending on the size of the mini-congregation.

The articles that follow in this volume present a variety of views about congregational size and transitions. The authors may disagree with each other on various points. Do not expect consistency. But look instead for insights that further develop a theory that is still under construction.

NOTES

1. Arlin J. Rothauge, *Sizing Up a Congregation for New Member Ministry* (New York: Seabury Press, for The Education and Ministry Office of the Episcopal Church, undated). The Rev. Arlin J. Rothauge, Ph.D., is founding director of Seabury Institute and professor of congregational studies, Seabury-Western Theological Seminary in Evanston, Illinois.
2. Ibid., p. 5.
3. Ibid., p. 5.
4. Arlin J. Rothauge, *A Church Is Born: Basics for Starting and Developing a Mission Congregation* (New York: Education for Mission and Ministry, The Episcopal Church Center, undated). Note that all Rothauge's books are undated. The year stated in the text is an estimate based on Rothauge's recollection and limited internal evidence in the books themselves.
5. Arlin J. Rothauge, *Reshaping a Congregation for a New Future* (New York: Education for Mission and Ministry, The Episcopal Church Center, undated).
6. Arlin J. Rothauge, *The Life Cycle in Congregations: A Process of Natural Creation and an Opportunity for New Creation* (New York: Congregational Development Services, The Episcopal Church Center, undated).
7. Arlin J. Rothauge, *Parallel Development: A Pathway for Exploring Change and a New Future in Congregational Life* (New York: Congregational Development Services, The Episcopal Church Center, undated).
8. Arlin J. Rothauge, *Making Small Groups Effective: Notes on Fellowships, Home Cell Groups, and House Churches in the Episcopal Tradition* (New York: Congregational Development Services, The Episcopal Church Center, undated).
9. Arlin J. Rothauge, *All Doors Open: Congregational Strategies for Comprehensive Evangelism and Outreach* (New York: Congregational Development Services, The Episcopal Church Center, undated).
10. Rothauge, *Sizing Up a Congregation*, p. 5.
11. Theodore William Johnson, *Congruence and Transitions in Congregational Size* (Evanston, Ill.: A thesis submitted to the faculty of Seabury-Western Theological Seminary in partial fulfillment of the requirements for the doctor of ministry in Congregational Development, 2000).
12. Malcolm Gladwell, *The Tipping Point: How Little Things Can Make a Big Difference* (Boston: Little, Brown and Company, 2000).
13. C. J. Buys and K. L. Larsen, "Human Sympathy Groups," *Psychology Reports* 45 (1979): 547-53 (cited by Gladwell).
14. R. I. M. Dunbar, "Neocortex size as a constraint on group size in primates," *Journal of Human Evolution* 20 (1992): 469-93 (cited by Gladwell).

CHAPTER 2

How to Minister Effectively in Family, Pastoral, Program, and Corporate Sized Churches

Roy M. Oswald

The theory of congregational size that I find most workable is Arlin Rothauge's, described in his booklet *Sizing Up a Congregation for New Member Ministry*.[1] It was originally written to help congregations recognize the ways different-sized churches assimilate new members. When a theory is on target, however, it so accurately reflects reality that it can be applied to other dimensions of a church's life and work. Rothauge's theory elicits consistent "ahas" from clergy who are reflecting on their transition from one size parish to another. Whether churches are growing or downsizing, congregations hold on to deeply ingrained assumptions about what constitutes a dynamic church and what effective clergy do. The inflexibility of these expectations is an important cause of clergy malfunctioning.

Rothauge sets forth four basic congregational sizes. Each size requires a specific cluster of behaviors from its clergy. The average number of people attending weekly worship and the amount of money being contributed regularly provide the most accurate gauge of church size. Since membership rolls fluctuate wildly depending on how frequently they are evaluated, they cannot provide an accurate measurement of congregational size. Rothauge also holds that a church's size category is a matter of attitude as much as numbers. I knew of one congregation that averaged 700 at Sunday worship and still functioned on a pastoral-size model. All the pastor did was preach on Sunday and visit people through the week. The pastor's perception of his job burned him out and eventually cost him his marriage and his ministry.

Here is a brief description of each of Rothauge's four sizes and my understanding of what members expect of clergy in each size.

THE PATRIARCHAL/MATRIARCHAL CHURCH:
UP TO FIFTY ACTIVE MEMBERS

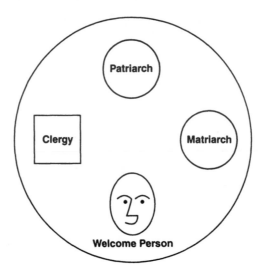

This small church can also be called a family-size church because it functions like a family, with appropriate parental figures. The patriarchs and matriarchs control the church's leadership needs. What family-size churches want from clergy is pastoral care, period. For clergy to assume that they are also the chief executive officer and the resident religious authority is to make a serious blunder. The key role of the patriarch or matriarch is to see that clergy do not take the congregation off on a new direction of ministry. Clergy are to be the chaplain of this small family. When clergy do not understand this, they are likely to head into a direct confrontation with the parental figure. It is generally suicide for clergy to get caught in a showdown with the patriarchs and matriarchs within the first five years of ministry at that particular church.

Clergy should not assume, however, that they have no role beyond pastoral care. In addition to providing quality worship and home or hospital visitation, clergy can play an important role as consultants to these patriarchs or matriarchs, befriending these parental figures and working alongside them, yet recognizing that when these parental figures decide against an idea, it is finished.

Clergy should watch out for the trap set when members complain to them about the patriarch or matriarch of the parish and encourage the pastor to challenge the parental figure. Clergy who respond to such mutinous bids, expecting the congregation to back them in the showdown, do not understand the dynamics of small-church ministry. The high turnover of clergy in these parishes has taught members that in the long run they have to live with old Mr. Schwartz who runs the feed mill, even if they do not like him. It is far too risky for members to get caught siding with pastors who come and go against their resident patriarch or matriarch.

Because these congregations usually cannot pay clergy an acceptable salary, many clergy see them as stepping stones to more rewarding opportunities. It is not unusual for a congregation of this size to list five successive clergy for every ten years of congregational life. As Lyle Schaller claims, the longer the pastorates, the more powerful clergy become. The shorter the pastorates, the more powerful the laity become. These family-size churches have to develop one or two strong lay leaders at the center of their life. How else would they manage their ongoing existence through those long vacancies and through the short pastorates of the ineffective clergy who are often sent their way?

The founder and past president of the Alban Institute, Loren Mead, began his ministry in a family-size church in South Carolina. Later in his ministry he attended a clergy conference at which he discovered seven other clergy who had also started their ordained ministry in the same parish. As they talked, those clergy realized that, in view of the difference in their styles and the shortness of their tenures, the only way that parish survived was to take none of them seriously.

One of the worst places to go right out of seminary is to a patriarchal/ matriarchal church. Seminarians are up to their eyeballs in new theories and good ideas. They want to see if any of them work. Even though some of those good ideas might be the ticket to their small church's long-term growth and development, the church's openness to trying any of them is next to zero. Sometimes, through the sheer force of personal persuasion, a pastor will talk a congregation into trying a new program or two. Pretty soon parishioners find themselves coming to church events much more than they really need to or want to. As they then begin to withdraw their investment from these new programs, the clergy inevitably take it personally. Concluding that their gifts for ministry are not really valued in this place, they begin to seek a call elsewhere. On the way out of the church they give it a kick, letting the parish know in subtle ways that they are a miserable example of Christian community.

These small congregations have endured such recriminations for decades. The message they get from their executive is that they are a failure because they fail to grow while consuming inordinate amounts of time. Middle judicatories try to merge them, yoke them, and close them—mostly to no avail. You can not kill these congregations with a stick. Large churches are far more vulnerable. An executive can place an incompetent pastor in a large church and lose 200 members in one year. Yet the same executive can throw incompetent clergy at family-size churches, leave them vacant for years, ignore them—all with little effect. The family-size church has learned to survive by relying on its own internal leadership.

These congregations need a pastor to stay and love them for at least ten years. This pastor would have to play by the rules and defer to the patriarch's or matriarch's leadership decisions for the first three to five years. At about year four or five the congregation might find itself in somewhat of a crisis. At some level they would be saying, "What do you mean you are going to stay? No clergy stay here. There must be something the matter with you." Then the questioning might begin: "Can we really trust you? No! You are going to leave us like all the rest." In this questioning we can see the pain of these congregations. Let us put ourselves in their shoes and imagine an ordained leader walking out on us every few years, berating us on the way out. Would we invest in the next pastor who came to us? Not likely! It would simply be too painful. The family-size church may have invested in one five years ago, only to find that the pastor left just when things started to move. Basically these people have learned not to trust clergy who repeatedly abandon ship when they see no evidence of church growth.

I conclude that we need to refrain from sending these congregations seminary trained pastors. History demonstrates that these churches have not been served well by full-time ordained clergy. Some judicatories have experimented with using people who already belong to the community. I believe long-term tent-making ministries offer the best possibility for ministering to many of these patriarchal/matriarchal churches. If denominations and middle judicatories persist in placing newly ordained clergy in these parishes, they should do so only after laying out this theory for these clergy, helping them discover who indeed are the patriarchs and matriarchs of the parish, and suggesting some strategies for working with them. If these clergy find it simply too difficult to work with these parental figures, they need to let their executive know promptly. Rather than leaving these newly ordained clergy regretting that they pursued ordained ministry in the first place, the executive should move them out of the family-size church.

THE PASTORAL-SIZE CHURCH: 50 TO 150 ACTIVE MEMBERS

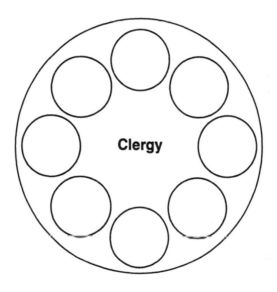

Clergy are usually at the center of a pastoral-size church. There are so many parental figures around that they need someone at the center to manage them. A leadership circle, made up of the pastor and a small cadre of lay leaders, replaces the patriarchs and matriarchs of the family-size church. The power and effectiveness of the leadership circle depends upon good communication with the congregation and the ability of the pastor to delegate authority, assign responsibility, and recognize the accomplishments of others. Without such skill, the central pastoral function weakens the entire structure. The clergyperson becomes overworked, isolated, exhausted, and may be attacked by other leaders. Finally, the harmony of the fellowship circle degenerates.

A key feature of a pastoral-size church is that laity experience having their spiritual needs met through their personal relationship with a seminary-trained person. In a pastoral-size church it would be rare for a Bible study or a prayer group to meet without the pastor. The pastor is also readily available in times of personal need and crisis. If a parishioner called the pastor and indicated that she needed some personal attention, the pastor would drop over to see her, probably that afternoon but certainly within the week—a qualitatively different experience from being told that the first available appointment to see the pastor in her office is two weeks from now. The time demands on the pastor of a pastoral-size church can become oppressive. However, most members will respond with loyalty to a reasonable level of attention and guidance from this central figure.

A second feature of the pastoral-size church is its sense of itself as a family in which everyone knows everyone else. If you show up at church with your daughter Julie by the hand, everyone will greet you and Julie, too. When congregations begin to have 130 to 150 people coming every Sunday morning, they begin to get nervous. As Carl Dudley put it,[2] they begin to feel "stuffed." Members wonder about the new faces they do not know—people who do not know them. Are they beginning to lose the intimate fellowship they prize so highly?

Clergy also begin to feel stressed when they have more than 150 active members whom they try to know in depth. In fact, this is one of the reasons why clergy may keep the pastoral-size church from growing to the next larger size—the program-size church. If clergy have the idea firmly fixed in their head that they are ineffective as a pastor unless they can relate in a profound and personal way with every member of the parish, then 150 active members (plus perhaps an even larger number of inactive members) are about all one person can manage.

There are some clergy who function at their highest level of effectiveness in the pastoral-size church. Given the different clusters of skills required for other sizes of congregations, some clergy should consider spending their entire career in this size congregation. Since the pastoral-size church can offer a pastor a decent salary, clergy tend to stick around longer. If clergy can regard themselves as successful only when they become pastor of a larger congregation, then sixty-five percent of mainline Protestant clergy are going to end their careers with feelings of failure. Two-thirds of mainline Protestant congregations are either family- or pastoral-size churches.

Clergy with strong interpersonal skills fare well in the pastoral-size church. These clergy can feed continually on the richness of direct involvement in the highs and lows of people's lives. Clergy who enjoy being at the center of most activities also do well. There are lots of opportunities to preach and lead in worship and to serve as primary instructors in many class settings for both young and old. Outgoing, expressive people seem to be the best matches for the style of ministry in the pastoral-size church. An open, interactive leadership style also seems to suit this size church best.

Growth in the pastoral-size church will depend mainly on the popularity and effectiveness of the pastor. People join the church because they like the interaction between pastor and people. When new people visit the congregation for the first time, it is likely to be the pastor who will make the follow-up house call.

When a congregation grows to the point that its pastor's time and energy is drawn off into many other activities and the one-on-one pastoral relationship begins to suffer, it may hire additional staff to handle these new functions, so the pastor can once again have plenty of time for interpersonal caring. Unfortunately, this strategy will have limited success. To begin with, when additional staff are hired, a multiple-staff organization has been created, which requires staff meetings, supervision, delegation, evaluation, and planning. These activities draw the pastor deeper into administration. Also, additional staff members tend to specialize in such things as Christian education, youth ministry, evangelism, or stewardship, which tends to add to the administrative role of the head of staff rather than freeing up his or her time for pastoral care.

Clergy consider a congregation's transition from pastoral- to program-size the most difficult. One can expect enormous resistance on the part of a pastoral-size church as it flirts with becoming a program-size church. Many churches make an unconscious choice not to make the transition and keep hovering around the level of 150 active members. The two treasured features of a pastoral-size church that will be lost if it becomes a program-size church are ready access to their religious leaders and the feeling of oneness as a church family, where everyone knows everyone else and the church can function as a single community.

Two things can prevent a congregation from making that transition. The first barrier is found in the clergy. When clergy hold on to a need to be connected in depth to all the active members, they become the bottlenecks to growth. The second barrier is found in the lay leaders who are unwilling to have many of their spiritual needs met by anyone except their ordained leader.

It is most helpful to put this theory up on newsprint before the chief decision-making body of the church and ask where it thinks the parish stands. If they have been saying "yes, yes" to church growth with their lips, but "no, no" with their behavior, this theory can be used to bring their resistance to the conscious level by pointing out the real costs they will face by growing. Churches tend to grow when parish leaders, fully aware of the cost of growth, make a conscious decision to proceed.

Without the backing of key lay leaders, the cost of moving from a pastoral- to program-size church usually comes out of the pastor's hide. The parish may welcome the pastor's efforts in parish program development, while still expecting all the parish calling and one-on-one work to continue at the same high level as before. Burnout or a forced pastoral termination can result.

The Program-Size Church:
150 to 350 Members

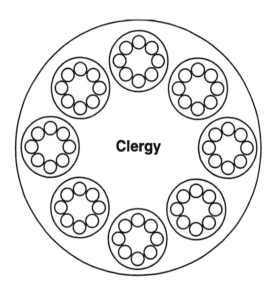

The program-size church grows out of the necessity for a high-quality personal relationship with the pastor to be supplemented by other avenues of spiritual feeding. Programs must now begin to fill that role.

The well-functioning program-size church has many cells of activity, which are headed up by lay leaders. These lay leaders, in addition to providing structure and guidance for these cells, also take on some pastoral functions. The stewardship committee gathers for its monthly meeting, and the committee chair asks about a missing member. Upon being told that Mary Steward's daughter had to be taken to the hospital for an emergency operation, the chair will allow time for expressions of concern for Mary and her daughter. The chair may include both of them in an opening prayer. If the teacher of an adult class notices that someone in the class is feeling depressed, the teacher will often take the class member aside and inquire about his well-being. Even if the teacher eventually asks the pastor to intervene, the pastor has already gotten a lot of assistance from this lay leader.

Clergy are still at the center of the program-size church, but their role shifts dramatically. Much of their time and attention is spent in planning with other lay leaders to ensure the highest quality programs. The pastor must spend a lot of time recruiting people to head up these smaller ministries, training, supervising, and evaluating them, and seeing to it that their morale remains high. In essence the pastor must often step back from direct ministry with people to coordinate and support volunteers who offer this ministry. Unless the pastor gives high priority to the spiritual and pastoral needs of lay leaders, those programs will suffer.

To be sure, a member can expect a hospital or home call from the pastor when personal crisis or illness strikes. But members had better not expect this pastor to have a lot of time to drink coffee in people's kitchens. To see the pastor about a parish matter, they will probably have to make an appointment at the church office several weeks in advance.

When clergy move from a pastoral- to program-size church, they will experience tension and difficulty in their new congregation unless they are ready to shift from a primarily interpersonal mode to a program planning and development mode. It is not that clergy will have no further need for their interpersonal skills. Far from it—they need to depend on them even more. But now those interpersonal skills will be placed at the service of the parish program.

Key skills for effective ministry in a program-size church begin with the ability to pull together the diverse elements of the parish into a mission statement. Helping the parish arrive at a consensus about its direction is essential. Next the pastor must be able to lead the parish toward attaining the goals that arise out of that consensus. To wilt in the face of opposition to this consensus will be seen as a lack of leadership ability. The program-size church pastor will also need to be able to motivate the most capable laypeople in the parish to take on key components of the parish vision and help make the vision become reality. Developing the trust and loyalty of these parish leaders and ensuring their continued spiritual growth and development is another key part of the cluster of skills needed in the program-size church.

For clergy who get their primary kicks out of direct pastoral care work, ministry in a program-size church may leave them with a chronic feeling of flatness and lack of fulfillment. Unless these clergy can learn to derive satisfaction from the work of pastoral administration, they should think twice about accepting a call to a parish of this size.

THE CORPORATE-SIZE CHURCH: 350 OR MORE ACTIVE MEMBERS

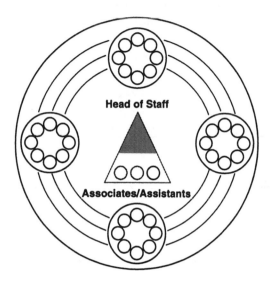

The quality of Sunday morning worship is the first thing you usually notice in a corporate-size church. Because these churches usually have abundant resources, they will usually have the finest organ and one of the best choirs in town. A lot of work goes into making Sunday worship a rich experience. The head of staff usually spends more time than other clergy preparing for preaching and leading worship.

In very large corporate-size churches, the head of staff may not even remember the names of many parishioners. When members are in the hospital, it is almost taken for granted that they will be visited by an associate or assistant pastor, rather than the senior pastor. Those who value highly the corporate-size church experience are willing to sacrifice a personal connection with the senior pastor in favor of the corporate-size church's variety and quality of program offerings.

Sometimes the head pastor is so prominent that the pastor acquires a legendary quality, especially in the course of a long pastorate. Few may know this person well, but the role does not require it. The head pastor becomes a symbol of unity and stability in a very complicated congregational life.

The corporate-size church is distinguished from the program-size church by its complexity and diversity. The patriarchs and matriarchs return, but now as members of the governing boards who formally, not just informally, control the church's life and future. Laity lead on many levels, and the corporate-size church provides opportunity to move up the ladder of influence.

Key to the success of the corporate-size church is the multiple staff and its ability to manage the diversity of its ministries in a collegial manner. Maintaining energy and momentum in a corporate-size church is very difficult when there is division within the parish staff. Any inability to work together harmoniously is especially evident during Sunday worship, when any tensions among the ordained leadership of the parish will manifest themselves in subtle ways.

It is at this point that clergy making the transition to the corporate-size church find themselves most vulnerable and unsupported. Our denominational systems do little to equip clergy to work collegially within a multiple staff. A three-day workshop on working with multiple staff is a bare introduction. Leaders in industry with master's degrees in personnel management still make serious mistakes in hiring and developing leaders for the corporation. The head of staff of a corporate-size church learns to manage a multiple staff by trial and error. Sacrificing a few associate and assistant clergy on the altar of experience is the price the church pays for such lack of training.

For the most part clergy are not taught to work collegially. In seminary we compete with one another for grades. Each of us retreats to his or her own cubicle to write term papers. There is little interaction in class. In seminary we do not really have to take each other seriously. This might change if, for example, a professor were to assign four seminarians to complete research on a church doctrine, write one paper, and receive a group grade. In that kind of learning atmosphere we would have to take one another on and argue about our different theological perspectives and forms of piety. Unless our training can begin to equip us for collegial ministry, our seminaries will continue to turn out lone rangers who do not really have to work with other clergy until they get to the corporate- or program-size church.

Clergy who are called as head of staff in corporate-size churches are usually multiskilled people who have proven their skill in a great variety of pastoral situations. In a multiple staff, however, the senior minister will need to delegate some of those pastoral tasks to other full-time staff members, who will inevitably want to do them differently. Learning to allow these people to do things their own way is in itself a major new demand.

Our research with the Myers-Briggs Type Indicator shows that congregations are best served when the multiple staff includes different types. The more diverse the staff, the greater its ability to minister to a diverse congregation. But this requirement for diversity makes multiple staff functioning more complicated. The more diverse the staff, the harder it is to understand and support one another's ministries.

Lay leaders are generally completely baffled by the inability of ordained people to work collegially. "If our religious leaders are not able to get along, what hope is there for this world?" they may wonder. Lay leaders could help enormously by seeing to it that there is money in the budget for regular consultative help for the staff. This help is not needed only when tensions arise. Multiple staffs need to be meeting regularly with an outside consultant to keep lines of communication open and difficulties surfaced.

When the multiple staff is having fun working well together, this graceful interaction becomes contagious throughout the corporate-size church. Lay people want to get on board and enjoy the camaraderie. The parish has little difficulty filling the many volunteer jobs needed to run the church.

In addition to learning to manage a multiple staff, clergy making the transition to head of staff need to hone their administrative skills. These clergy are becoming chief executive officers of substantial operations. Yet I would emphasize leadership skills over management skills. While managers can manage the energy of a parish, leaders can generate energy. The corporate-size church needs leaders who know how to build momentum. Otherwise, even when managed well, these large churches run out of gas and begin to decline.

In summary, the most difficult transitions in size are from pastoral to program size or when downsizing, from program to pastoral size. These are two very different ways to be church. More is required than a theoretical vision of the shift. We need to deal with the fact that a shift in size at this level just does not feel right to people. Somewhere deep inside they begin to sense that "it does not feel like church" anymore.

CHOICE POINTS FOR CLERGY:
A GROUP EXERCISE

Because the movement from one size to another is so difficult, it is not uncommon for parishioners to want to add a hundred new members to the parish but be unwilling to change anything about their parish to accommodate the increase. We often refer to this as the vampire theory of growth: "We need some new blood around here." Basically members desire a bunch of new people to help pay the bills and to fill up the choir, Sunday school, and sanctuary, but they do not expect to make any sacrifices related to the things they want from their church.

Some of the greatest upheaval caused by numerical growth occurs when a congregation is on the borderline between any two of the sizes of congregations described earlier. When a congregation crosses the boundary between one size and another, it needs to begin relating to its clergy in ways that might be radically different from their previous ways of relating to the pastor.

To review these descriptions in a group setting, ask four volunteers each to summarize the dynamics of one of the four types of congregations. At the end of each summary ask group members if they remember any additional points. Fill in any important aspects not brought up. Briefly discuss which description best suits your parish.

Remind the group that the most difficult transitions are between the pastoral- and program-size churches. The following activity will help illustrate what a transition from one size church to the other might mean.

Ask participants to stand and push the chairs to the side of the room, clearing the floor.

Rather than have participants simply circle answers to prepared questions, I like to send the A's to one side of the room and the B's to the other side. You can see at a glance where everyone stands on an issue, and the two groups can talk to each other about their choices. Because the questions deal with choices clergy need to make between two competing activities, I ask any clergy present to remain silent until the other participants have answered.

Decide where in the room the people who choose A responses will gather and where those who choose B will stand. Read aloud one set of A-B choices. Have participants indicate their responses by going to the designated place in the room. Tally the results. Allow up to two minutes for the two groups to discuss their stance, then go on to the next question.

Each set of questions represents a choice point for your pastor. Imagine your pastor has had a week full of crises and has only limited time left. Which response represents your preference for what the pastor should do?

A. Visit more shut-ins?
B. Prepare a better sermon?

A. Attend a wedding reception?
B. Go on a retreat with parish staff?

A. Call on prospective members?
B. Conduct a training session for church officers?

A. Visit a bereaved family?
B. Help two church officers resolve a conflict?

A. Make a hospital call on a fringe member?
B. Attend a continuing education event?

A. Give pastoral counseling to members?
B. Attend a planning event with officers?

A. Call on parishioners?
B. Recruit leaders for parish events?

A. Attend an activity with parish youth?
B. Critique a meeting with a church officer?

Once you have completed the exercise as a group, invite the pastor to share personal responses to each question. I encourage clergy to choose the activity they would most enjoy rather than the one they believe might claim a higher parish priority. The differences between the pastor's and laity's responses to these questions might result in some fruitful discussion related to size of congregation and pastoral expectations.

This activity can point out several issues:

1. Congregations may be program size yet still require their clergy to attend to all the category A pastoral activities. This is a perfect prescription for burnout. It can also lead to labeling clergy as "bad"

because they do not accomplish all the tasks in the A column while they are also expected to crank out quality programs for the parish (category B activities).

2. Clergy in small pastoral-size churches should be focusing their energies and attention on the A activities. But sometimes because their background or training is in program-size churches, they continue to concentrate on the B activities or feel guilty because they are not doing so.

3. Clergy and laity often disagree on priorities for clergy. This exercise often surfaces those differences quickly and makes role negotiation possible.

Clergy may be set up for failure when they move from effective work in one size congregation and begin a new pastorate in a congregation of another size. If, for example, a pastor is thriving in a pastoral-size congregation and then receives a call to a program-size congregation, the pastor will have to make a significant shift in ministry style to be effective in the new congregation. Because not only clergy but also members get stuck at each size, every time there is a shift in size, clergy need to help the congregation's leaders understand that they also need to change their behavior. The failure to grow is rarely a conscious decision on the part of either pastor or congregation. Unless both are willing to make the sometimes painful changes needed to become a new size, however, the pastor and congregation will almost certainly minister less effectively than those who understand how size affects the style of ministry and make the needed adaptations.

NOTES

1. Arlin J. Rothauge, *Sizing Up a Congregation for New Member Ministry*, available from The Episcopal Church Center, 815 Second Avenue, New York, NY 10017.

2. Carl Dudley, *Unique Dynamics of the Small Church* (Washington, D.C.: The Alban Institute, 1977).

Adapted from Roy Oswald, "Changing Sizes of Congregations," in Making Your Church More Inviting *(Washington, D.C.: The Alban Institute, 1992).*

CHAPTER 3

What Happens Between Sizes?

Why Congregations Get Stuck

Alice Mann

FAULT LINES

My brother used to live near the San Andreas fault in California. The San Andreas is a long rift in the earth's crust that periodically tears open to accommodate shifts in the two tectonic plates whose meeting creates a fault line. As a visitor to my brother's home, I used to imagine myself standing with one foot on each side of the fault, then dropping into a chasm when the earthquake hit.

Size transition is a lot like standing on the fault line. Churches moving through the plateau zones on the graph below are actually crossing fault lines on this topographical map. You can make better decisions if you know not only where the rifts occur but also what deeper movements of the earth are driving the surface eruption. Congregations are changing and adjusting all the time. Dozens of different factors are in play, and subtle gradations exist that make any size theory look oversimplified. Still, some of the forces at work are more powerful than others, more determinative of relationships and results. For the majority of congregations,[1] a two-dimensional model of size change will clarify the lines of demarcation.

One dimension of change, shown along the bottom of the following chart, is described by the terms *organism* and *organization*. The other dimension is described by the terms *pastor-centered* and *group-centered*. As congregations move among Rothauge's four sizes—family, pastoral, program, and corporate—they follow an N-shaped path across the fault lines.

Size Transition "N-Curve"

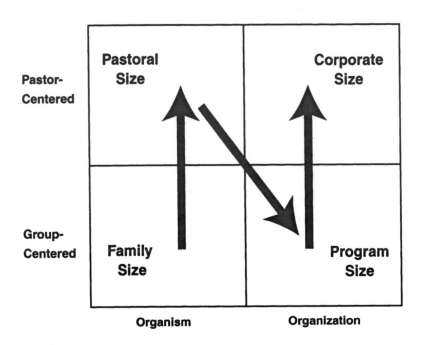

ORGANISM VERSUS ORGANIZATION

Family- and pastoral-size churches resemble an organism more than an organization. Congregations of these two sizes tend to be relatively homogeneous in make-up. Each revolves around a central relationship that can be immediately and intuitively apprehended: the relationship among members as a "primary group" or "single cell" (family-size church) or the dyadic relationship between the sole ordained leader and the congregation (pastoral-size church). The congregation's identity is largely inherent in these central relationships. Ask the question "Who are you as a church?" in a family-size congregation, and someone will probably introduce you around the whole circle of members. Ask that question in a pastoral-size church, and someone will most likely tell you about the congregation's relationship with its pastor, often symbolized by the rapport (or lack thereof) between pastor and board. In these two smaller sizes, the notion that a congregation might choose or shape an identity intentionally would probably seem odd; identity is more of a given, to be preserved and defended.

In program- and corporate-size churches, on the other hand, the variety and complexity of relationships require conscious attention to matters of identity, purpose, structure, role of leaders, and so on. Neither the members nor the pastor can intuitively grasp the wholeness of the system. The larger membership and the rich variety of programming will only cohere well if leaders construct a clear identity for the church—often expressed in a mission statement, a vision, or a strategic plan. For people raised in smaller churches, this work of construction may seem taxing and bureaucratic. On the other hand, the quest for intentionality typical of a larger congregation might stimulate their imagination about church life, clarify their reasons for participation, and provide richer networks of friendship, growth, and ministry. Membership is more of a choice than a given.

The distinction between organism and organization is not absolute. Small congregations are still subject to the laws that govern not-for-profit corporations in the United States and may be vulnerable to lawsuits if they do not attend well to organizational matters like the employment, accountability, and termination of staff. Larger congregations are still living systems, held together by subtly balanced forces that we may only dimly perceive. Nevertheless, the difference between the two emphases is usually palpable.

GROUP-CENTERED VERSUS PASTOR-CENTERED

The movement from family- to pastoral-size (the upward arrow on the left-hand side of the previous chart) involves a change in the way the system centers its life. The family-size church feels like a tribe or a committee of the whole. Not everyone on the committee has equal influence, to be sure, but the single cell of members works things through in its own characteristic way. A student minister or part-time pastor who tries to take charge of that cell is in for a rude awakening, because a family-size church does not generally revolve around the pastor.[2]

At a worship attendance of about 35 people, the single cell of membership becomes stretched. By the time it hits 50, the unbroken circle of members—the defining constellation of the congregation's life—is in crisis. In order to increase further, the system must allow itself to become a multi-celled organism, holding together two or three overlapping networks of family and fellowship, and it must establish a symbolic center around which those multiple cells can orient themselves. Typically, it becomes pastor-centered.

A great deal has been written about the dangers of clerical domination in churches, and many have questioned whether this shift to a pastor-centered system is desirable at all. I would not equate "pastor-centered" with "pastor-dominated." The research of Speed Leas and George Parsons suggests that a greater proportion of members may actually participate in decisions at pastoral size than at family size.[3] It may be that the heightened role of the pastor in relation to the board moves the congregation's political center from the kitchen table to a more accessible public setting and requires that the ordained and elected leaders work as a team to move projects forward. The pastor's central position as communication switchboard also allows for a great deal of informal consultation and problem solving; he or she can monitor key relationships, initiate needed conversations, and anticipate likely clashes.

As attendance approaches 150, however, the congregation must become more group-centered once again, because the pastor can no longer carry the whole system in his or her head. There are too many individual pastoral needs to track. The relationships among projects and leaders are becoming too complex to be coordinated solely through board discussion and pastoral diplomacy. A new kind of teamwork becomes necessary in an uneven leadership matrix in which some programs have paid staff, some have volunteer leaders so dedicated that they function like staff, and some have committees at the helm. Board and pastor must find ways to keep the parts connected with each other directly—in horizontal networks of collaboration—not just indirectly through board reports and liaisons. As in a spider web, the center of this leadership network does not consist of a single point (the pastor) but of a small circle (half a dozen key program leaders—paid and unpaid, clergy and lay) led by the pastor.

In the move to program size, clergy must shift a good deal of their time and attention away from the direct delivery of pastoral care and focus on assembling and guiding the small team of program leaders. They must also find ways to offer spiritual enrichment to the board, whose job has become much more demanding. Skills for this kind of group-oriented ministerial leadership have not usually been emphasized in seminary or employed as primary selection criteria in the ordination process. Hence, many clergy find themselves poorly equipped for a pastoral-to-program transition.

To make things worse, the breakdown of the pastor-centered way of being a church occurs at the same time as the shift from organism to organization. The congregation is now traversing the diagonal portion of the N-shaped path, crossing both the horizontal and vertical fault lines simultaneously. The pastoral-to-program change is doubly discontinuous.

When attendance reaches about 350, the need for more pastor-centered leadership emerges once again. (Note the vertical line on the right-hand side of the chart.) The program-size church's lively but lumpy network of staff, volunteer program heads, and committees can no longer provide the overview and strategic direction the system needs. At corporate size, complex networks of coordination are still required, but the central pastor must begin to project a large enough symbolic presence—through preaching, presiding, leading the board, and heading the expanded staff—to unify a diverse and energetic community. To be effective, this high-profile leader must find a reliable way to maintain spiritual perspective and must use the aura of leadership to help the whole system grapple with its core identity and purpose.

Six Transitions

It may be helpful to summarize some critical issues that must be addressed during the six possible transitions within the Rothauge framework.

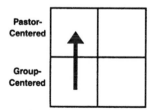

Family-to-Pastoral Transition

- Loss of self-esteem by matriarchs and patriarchs as they lose decisive influence in the system: Can they with help pass the mantle, while maintaining pride in past accomplishments?

- Tendency for unseasoned clergy to take resistance personally: How can congregations find mature pastoral leadership? How can less experienced clergy find mentors to help them handle their own insecurities?

- Reluctance to divide the single cell: How can current leadership weigh what may be gained and lost as they relinquish the expectation that every event (Sunday worship, study programs, Christmas Eve service) must include the whole family?

- Financial realism: Clergy salaries and benefits are rising in most denominations. Can the congregation move solidly enough into pastoral size to attain stability?

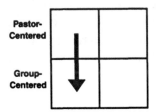

Pastoral-to-Family Transition

- Loss of self-esteem by congregation when it feels it is no longer operating like a "real" church: Will the move signal slow death, or will something new and vigorous begin?

- Ministry development: How will gifts be discerned and developed for a rich variety of homegrown ministries?

- Support and accountability: How will the family-size church partner with its denomination (or with parachurch organizations) to monitor the development of sound ministries and open channels to other congregations, leaders, and ideas?

- Physical plant: What is an appropriate facility for the church? Does worship need to be moved, so that the space will be at least half full on Sunday (the minimum required to attract newcomers)?

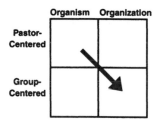

Pastoral-to-Program Transition

- Clergy role: Will leaders recognize the double messages they are giving the clergy about what they expect? (Try the "A-B" exercise in chapter 2.) Will clergy work on resolving their personal ambivalence about these choices and on gaining the new skills they need? How will staff be augmented to allow for growth?

- Program leadership: How will gifted and motivated people be selected, equipped, and authorized to serve as department heads? Does the pastor have the skills needed to forge these leaders into a staff team? Who will help the average member identify gifts for ministry (inside and outside the congregation), and who will make sure that every form of volunteer service to the congregation is a spiritually rewarding experience?

- Communication: How can people involved in implementing different programs stay personally connected with leaders from other programs? Will formal information channels (newsletter, bulletin, spoken announcements, telephone trees) be improved and intensified, so that timely, accurate, and thorough communication is the norm?

- Democratic participation: What channels will be provided so that every member can have a say and a stake in the shape of church life? How will members remain aware of, and accountable to, a central purpose?

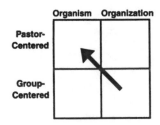

Program-to-Pastoral Transition

- Reshaping expectations: How will the congregation refocus on a few central strengths? Will attention be given to the sense of loss and grief that may accompany a consolidation of energies?

- Clergy role: What satisfactions and status must the pastor relinquish? How will simpler patterns of pastoral care be established?

- Sunday morning: How can the worship and education schedule be made manageable without reinforcing a cycle of decline? Can the church maintain at least two worship options of somewhat different styles?

- Ministry development: Healthy pastoral-size churches still foster active lay leadership, especially in new-member incorporation, education, and community outreach. How will the pastor shift to a less formal style of delegation and mentoring? How will the number of committees be reduced in favor of small, hands-on ministry teams?

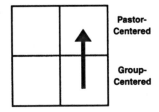

Program-to-Corporate Transition

- Depth and quality of programming: How will the church step up to a higher level of expectations? Do staff members need new position descriptions (focused on empowering others for ministry) and a definite plan to gain new skills?

- Symbolic presence of central pastor: Is the senior minister ready to step into a lonelier, more spiritually hazardous role? Will he or she put in place new disciplines such as regular spiritual guidance, adequate time for sermon preparation, and use of third-party help in planning, conflict resolution, and staff development? Who will mentor the central pastor around new and difficult responsibilities (personnel, endowment, delegation)?

- Strategic direction: In a system as hard to turn as an ocean liner, how will the senior pastor and the central board keep their focus on the big questions about the church's purpose and role? How will they engage the rest of the system in those questions without abdicating leadership?

- Small group connection: Will the congregation establish an excellent pattern of small group ministry through which members can connect faith with daily life? Will small group leaders be trained through apprenticeship, so that the more experienced leaders can constantly be forming new groups?

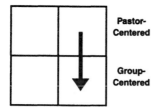

Pastor-Centered

Group-Centered

Corporate-to-Program Transition

- Relinquishing status: Will the church be honest about its decline and resist the temptation simply to keep up appearances?

- Use of endowment: Is the church steadily spending down the gifts of the past, rather than facing the need to consolidate programs and to develop a relevant approach to evangelism?

- Cavernous buildings: Does the sea of empty seats reinforce the cycle of decline and undermine the vitality that could be developed?

- Clergy role: Can the central pastor establish a more collegial relationship with the major program leaders and help the board to take back the spiritual leadership that may have been relinquished in the past to a small group of trustees?

In the case of impending transition to a smaller size, each congregation will need to assess its growth potential and outreach commitments. Do not reconfigure for the smaller size if you intend to move through the plateau zone within the next couple of years.

THE DOUBLE-MINDED CHURCH

A classic prayer asks for the grace to love and serve God "with gladness and singleness of heart." Both joy and single-mindedness start to run short in a size transition; they are replaced by profound ambivalence. Once a church has entered the plateau zone, the strength and appeal of the previous size are already compromised, while the virtues of the next size are not yet in place. Leaders find themselves in a lose-lose position, because two competing sets of expectations are laid upon them. Confusion, anxiety, and indecision often result.

Some of the most poignant passages in Exodus and Numbers describe the ambivalence of the faith community in its transition from the land of bondage to the land of promise. When the people first left Egypt, they were so daunted by their transitional circumstances that some of them wished aloud, "If only we had died by the hand of the Lord in the land of Egypt, when we sat by the fleshpots and ate our fill of bread" (Exod. 16:3).

Once they had received the Law and moved on from Sinai, they even began to remember Egypt as a place flowing with milk and honey—a description usually reserved for the promised land. Their attention constantly drifted from God's mighty acts to the most domestic of details: "We remember the fish we used to eat in Egypt for nothing, the cucumbers, the melons, the leeks, the onions, and the garlic; but now our strength is dried up, and there is nothing at all but this manna to look at" (Num. 11:5-6).

The following biblical reflection questions might help you get in touch with your own inner conflicts about size transition.

BIBLICAL REFLECTION

1. Read Numbers 10:33 to 11:9. Why do you think the passage from Numbers talks about food in such detail?
2. Can you imagine yourself wanting to go back to Egypt? Why or why not?
3. As your church considers issues of size transition, what do you already miss that might be comparable to the Israelites' longing for savory smells from their kitchens in Egypt?
4. If your congregation moved solidly to the next size (smaller or larger), what do you imagine to be the greatest loss you personally would have to deal with?

APPLICATION EXERCISE

1. Which, if any, of the six transitions discussed in this chapter is your church experiencing?
2. Review the critical issues that commonly accompany that particular transition. To what extent has your congregation encountered each of these issues? What other issues have you experienced as a result of your change in size?

NOTES

1. Those with an average attendance below 800.
2. There are exceptions to this observation. When a part-time pastor stays longer than a decade or so, or when endowment income has made it possible to retain a full-time pastor over the years, the dynamics of a family-size church begin to resemble, in many ways, those of a pastoral-size church.
3. Speed B. Leas and George D. Parsons, *Understanding Your Congregation as a System* (Washington, D.C.: The Alban Institute, 1993), p. 126.

From Alice Mann, The In-Between Church: Navigating Size Transitions in Congregations *(Bethesda, Md.: The Alban Institute, 1998).*

CHAPTER 4

Sizing Up a Congregation

How Size Affects Function

Douglas Alan Walrath

One sure way to start an argument among church leaders is to advocate as the best some particular way of categorizing congregations. Each person will usually rise quickly to champion his or her favorite: theological focus, denominational affiliation, type of community, size of congregation—and so the list goes.

I must admit that occasionally I fall into that trap, though most of the time I remember that a better way to clarify the nature and significance of differences among congregations is to employ several frames of reference. Frankly, I do not believe that any one way of looking at churches is inherently better than the rest. Usually I employ several when working with a congregation, for the same reason a physician uses more than one diagnostic tool. Each frame of reference yields different insights about why a congregation behaves as it does. So I choose the approaches that experience tells me will provide the particular insights I need to have.

I find church size to be one of the most useful frames of reference I can use when I am seeking to understand the internal dynamics of a congregation—styles of church organization, leadership, communication, and planning that are functional in that congregation.

For example, I reviewed the planning task force proposals of a very large, urban congregation with whom I planned to work. With supporting data, the report contained nearly 100 pages. Their plans were already a year in the making. A dozen obviously talented members of this congregation's planning task force had systematically and thoroughly studied their church and community; the carefully typed minutes they shared with me detailed their yearlong effort. Looking through their impressive work, I was tempted to generalize, "That's the way planning *ought* to be done!"

Yet, I know otherwise. While attending the annual meeting of another congregation I witnessed an equally impressive but very different approach. During consideration of the church's budget, the conversation strayed quite far from the printed agenda to a discussion of the widespread unemployment that afflicts the community served by this church of less than 80 members. It appeared that we were in for a long harangue as people shared their biases about the causes of that unemployment—until one man suggested the church do something to attack the problem.

"Maybe some of those people who 'won't' work don't know how to work. Maybe they have never had the opportunity to learn. Why don't we employ some of them in our housing ministry this summer?" (This church participated in a ministry of building and improving homes for the poor, handicapped, and other victims of misfortune in the community.) Within a few minutes, the congregation had agreed to try this approach, decided how to begin and who would guide the effort. Again I found myself saying, "That's the way planning *ought* to be done!"

The style of planning that will work best in a congregation is to some degree bound up with how large or small the church is. When we know what size a church is, quantitatively speaking, we also know that we can probably draw some qualitative conclusions about the way people will tend to function in that congregation. In the table that follows I have outlined some of those conclusions I have made based on my work in congregations as a pastor, church executive, and consultant. Let me suggest some cautions to keep in mind as you use the table.

The precise number of members I have indicated in connection with each size category can be misleading. Church rolls are notoriously inaccurate—especially in declining churches. The congregation you are seeking to understand may actually belong to a type larger or smaller than its enrolled membership would indicate. So, it may be more helpful to begin by considering one of the functional categories like "key characteristics" or "typical planning style" to appropriately place your congregation.

When congregations change in size they tend to continue to function in old ways. Thus a congregation that loses members may hold on to an organizational style that is too complex and large for its current needs; leaders may be unable to function effectively because so much of their energy is used up in maintaining an oversized organization. By contrast, a congregation that is growing often attempts to hold on to an informal organizational style that inhibits its ability to develop the number and variety of programs needed by its current membership. If your congregation has recently changed in size, are the ways you now function still appropriate?

Finally, avoid normative thinking—like "Bigger would be better." With congregations, bigger is not necessarily better; neither is smaller. Big and small are simply different. Employing styles of functioning in various aspects of your church's life that are appropriate for a church of your size will enhance the effectiveness of your leaders—and the ministries and mission of your church as well.

Organizational Types

	Very Small (Under 75 members; Average attendance: under 50)	Small (75-200 members; Average attendance: 40-100)	Middle-Size (200-350 members; Average attendance: 75-200)	Moderately Large (350-800 members; Average attendance: 150-400)	Very Large (Over 800 members; Average attendance: over 350)
Usual Size					
Key Characteristics	A tight-knit group	Familiar faces; dominant core group	Full-time pastor; full program	Diverse fellowship and program	Comprehensive program; specialized staff
Definition	A tight-knit group who have regular interaction with one another; one or two extended families may dominate. Very small congregations almost always have limited resources. They must limit programs to bare essentials and/or cooperate with other congregations to provide a full program and pastoral leadership.	A homogeneous group who all know about one another and who are dominated by a single core of leading members or families. Small churches usually have limited resources and must cooperate with others to employ clergy and to provide a full program.	A relatively homogeneous group who function within several subgroups around a single center and who are economically self-sufficient and able to provide a full program and support a full-time pastor.	A diverse association of individuals and groups sufficient in size to support a variety of programs that meet needs and interests both within and beyond the church membership. In addition to the pastor, the congregation usually employs at least part-time program staff.	A complex association of many individuals and groups who support a wide range of programs, professional staff, and facilities to meet their own needs and to reach out to others within the region the church serves.
Typical Pattern of Familiarity and Interaction	Members know and interact with one another regularly.	All members have current informaton about each other; a majority interact with one another regularly.	Pastor has current information about all members; a few members have current information about most. A nucleus, often a majority, interact with one another regularly; the rest interact primarily within subgroups.	Pastor has current information about almost all members. A core of members interact with one another regularly; a majority interact primarily within subgroups.	No single member or pastor has current information about all members. Regular interactions are confined largely to subgroups, even during such large gatherings as worship services.

Primary Organizational Roles of Lay and Clergy Leaders	A few people set the tone and direction of the group; often they hold the same offices and program responsibilities for many years. Roles of clergy limited to those functions prescribed by local traditions, required by denominational polity, and deemed essential by local leaders. Clergy seen almost entirely in preacher-pastoral role.	People within the nucleus exercise overall control. Even when formal leadership posts rotate among church members, those with real influence remain constant, guiding forces. The same people often carry the program responsibilities year after year. Lay leaders, tradition, and denominational polity set boundaries within which clergy must function. Clergy usually viewed primarily in a preacher-pastoral role.	People elected to board(s) determine policy and programs, with the influence of a few respected leaders. Lay people usually carry major responsibility for maintenance and finance, and share responsibility for programs with pastors in other areas. Pastor usually expected to provide direct guidance in all areas.	People elected to boards set policy and allocate program development responsibility to well-defined subgroups whose work they review at stated intervals. Lay people share responsibility for program delivery in many areas with pastor and other paid (usually part-time) staff. Pastor and other employed staff are expected to offer suggestions and guidance in their areas of expertise. Individual responsibilities are limited and defined.	People elected to boards and agencies set policy and direction. Various administrative, maintenance, and program functions are assigned to subgroups and usually coordinated by staff. Trained lay people share responsibility for delivery of services with employed staff, with staff usually playing key roles in each area. Pastors and other staff are expected to offer expertise and guidance within areas assigned to them.
Typical Communication System	Word of mouth.	Word of mouth, supplemented by print.	Word of mouth within the core group and subgroups, print to reach others.	Generally by print; word of mouth with subgroups and core groups.	Generally by print and other formal means; word of mouth with staff and subgroups.
Typical Planning Style	Spontaneous and informal; carried on within nucleus and based on data available to members' experience.	Usually spontaneous and informal; carried on by nucleus and based mostly on data available to members' experience.	Usually formal; carried on by board and pastor; sometimes with subgroups. Based on data available in group and occasionally on research.	Formal; carried on by board and assigned by subgroups. Pastor and other staff participate. Data often gathered by research.	Formal; carried on by subgroups coordinated by board, occasionally aided by consultants. Data usually gathered through a formal research process.

From Action Information *11, no. 3 (May/June 1985): pp. 7-10.*

CHAPTER 5

Leader Relationships

A Key to Congregational Size

Edward H. Koster

HOW WE COMMUNICATE

Every time we communicate with another human being, we communicate on two levels. The one we pay the most attention to is the transmission of information through words.

However, as we communicate with words, we are also communicating in other ways. These second-level ways of communicating involve such phenomena as voice quality, tone, and tempo, the way we sit or stand, or even the color of our skin. These we sometimes call body language. We frequently augment body language intentionally by the way we dress, the place we choose for communicating, or even the color of the room. At the conscious level, we are usually unaware of what is being communicated in those ways, though we are sometimes aware of feelings that are associated with the words we hear. When we find ourselves responding to certain words in a way that does not seem rational, it is often these subconscious messages that are affecting us.

The nonverbal element of communication does carry information, though not as precisely as the verbal component. It carries instructions from the speaker to the listener about the nature of the relationship between the speaker and the listener, and how the words are to be received. When a soldier hears, "This is an order," the relationship between the speaker and the listener is explicit. In order to avoid such obvious commands, we normally use more subtle forms of communication. This is the function of dress that identifies rank, seating arrangements, or even the size of an office or desk.

Paul Watzlawick, Janet Bavelas, and Don D. Jackson, in their book *The Pragmatics of Human Communication* (New York: W. W. Norton &

Company, 1967), developed a model to describe the relational level of human communication that has informed communication theory for decades. They call this model "meta communications," because it stands above, and communicates about, communication.

A significant element in the framework established by Watzlawick, Bavelas, and Jackson is the possibility of addressing communicational issues on two levels. For the most part, we tend to focus on the *content* of communication, the words—discussing, debating, and sometimes fighting over what has been said. In many cases, however, the real issue in communication is not the content, but the *relationship* between the parties.

Pragmatics (as opposed to semantics and syntactics) deal specifically with the meta levels of human communication, specifically, the establishment of relationships between people as they communicate with one another. Watzlawick, Bavelas, and Jackson conclude that only two types of relationships can be established between people. One they call "symmetrical," the other "complementary." Furthermore, they conclude that every communication between people specifies which relationship is operant, and that relationship is most frequently communicated nonverbally.

A symmetrical relationship is one in which the parties involved are on an equal level, with neither having priority over the other. The opinions or wishes of one have equal weight with those of the other. When the relationship is symmetrical, establishing the priority of one person's opinion over the opinions of another theoretically rests on the content of the information that is transferred. The outcome rests upon the "superiority" of one position over the other and the ability of one party to convince the other. This is the thesis behind debates, judicial proceedings, labor negotiations, and a host of other human communication.

Problems in human communication (and relations) occur when there is conflict. And it is in conflict that the relationship between parties becomes obvious. When the relationship is symmetrical, the first attempt to resolve conflicts is by the use of persuasion. When this fails, the parties often seek a compromise, in which each "wins" a little, and each "loses" a little. If compromise fails, then only two strategies remain. One is to seek arbitration. The arbitrator, from a meta position, makes choices on behalf of both parties. If arbitration fails or is not chosen, either the parties agree to disagree, or the conflict is escalated. The greatest danger in symmetrical relationships is escalation, because there are no built-in restraints.

A complementary relationship, the other possibility, assumes that one party has some kind of priority over the other. A complementary relationship is assumed in all hierarchical organizations. One person has priority over the other by virtue of position.

Significantly, in this kind of relationship the self-understanding of each party involved is bound up in the relationship itself. Person "A" understands him or herself to be the "one-up" (dominant) party. This is not possible unless there is another present who accepts the "one-down" (subordinate) role. The end result is that when difficulties occur in this kind of relationship, they are taken as a much more personal issue than in the symmetrical relationship. To challenge a person's one-up (or one-down) status is to challenge that person's self-concept. Conflicts that develop in this kind of relationship can be very destructive psychologically.

We need to describe how these relationships are carried out in the real world. First, the nature of the relationship is normally communicated in an implicit, usually nonverbal form. It can be seen in such issues as which person has the power to begin or end a series of communications. These are important questions: Who has the first word and the last word? Who has the power to bring up certain subjects, and who does not? Who has the option of interrupting another, and who does not?

Furthermore, because the message given and received is so subtle, we take it for granted. We tend to sense when there is no agreement as to the proper relationship by experiencing some kind of unpleasant feeling. Often, we cannot place labels on it except for words like "anxious" or "angry" or "uneasy."

The paradigm is complicated by a human factor. The truth is that even if equality (a symmetrical relationship) is embraced as the ideal, everyone tends to want to be a little more equal than the other person. So it turns out that a struggle for the one-up position is almost always present in human relationships, albeit sometimes on a very low-key level. In practice it is impossible to have communication in which some part is not complementary. Otherwise, no one would ever be able to initiate or to end a simple conversation.

Finally, it is very important to avoid placing any moral labels on the two kinds of relationships. One is not good and the other bad. The basic issue is not morality but propriety. What is the appropriate relationship in a specific context?

The intention of this chapter is to investigate the meta communication dynamics between the pastor and lay leader of a church. My specific thesis is that the type of relationship that exists between lay and clergy leaders significantly affects the size of the congregation.

CONGREGATIONAL SIZE

The congregational sizes I am using refer to the number of adults (thirteen years old and over) who attend services on an average Sunday morning. This is a more accurate way of categorizing churches by size, because the way members are counted varies so greatly among churches and denominations.

We will focus on two points on the spectrum of sizes and on the congregational dynamics that occur at these points. When we look at congregational growth, experience has shown that is very difficult for a growing congregation to move past attendance figures of 100, and again around 200. Congregations near these two points tend to get stuck on size plateaus. It is very hard to crack these levels permanently.[1]

The question is why? What is there about these two levels of participation that produces such resistance to growth? We believe that the paradigm suggested by Watzlawick, Bavelas, and Jackson provides a significant clue to the reason behind these points of resistance.

The issue revolves around the leaders in a congregation. Three basic kinds of leadership models seem to be possible. In one model the laity have the initiating power—the power to begin or end things. Depending on congregational style, this power can be held by an individual, a family, a special interest group, or some nonordained staff person (such as a choir director or a secretary).

In the second model the pastor or pastors have the initiating power. This occurs in congregations of 200 or more.

The third model holds that the initiating power is shared by the laity and the pastor, or that the power alternates between the laity and the pastor, depending upon the situation.

In terms of the relational communications identified by Watzlawick, Bavelas, and Jackson, the first and the second models of leadership (lay or pastoral) are predicated upon complementary relationships, the first with the laity one-up, the second with the pastor one-up. When there is some kind of shared leadership arrangement (model three), there is a symmetrical relationship between the pastor and the laity.

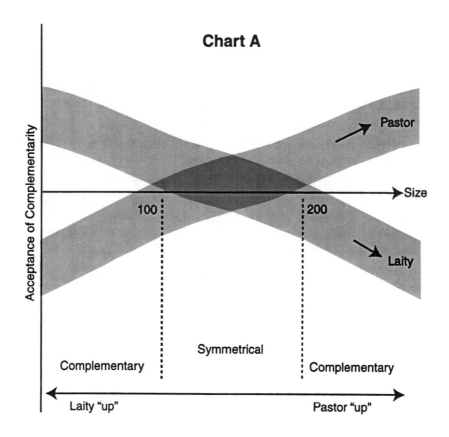

Chart A

The illustration in chart A shows how these relationships are played out according to the size of a congregation. The horizontal axis is the measure of a congregation's size. The two bands represent a spectrum of complementary communications, one representing the pastor, the other the lay leaders. These are represented by a spectrum, because no person communicates exclusively in one mode or the other. The vertical axis represents the degree of expectation that all the parties involved will accept the complementary relationship.

In churches ranging in size from very small to about 100, there is a clear expectation of a complementary relationship between the pastor and the lay leadership, with laity one-up. The pastor, in churches of this range, is not expected to be the initiating leader, but rather needs to be what Carl Dudley has so elegantly called a "lover." The laity make the decisions, and the pastor is often the last person to be informed of them. The pastor is expected to be occupied with visiting parishioners, calling on visitors, responding to crises. The clergy role focuses on pastoral care, rather than leadership.

The lay leader model becomes untenable when attendance approaches 100 because of the size and complexity of the organization. The leadership arrangements are too cumbersome and imprecise to cope with the increased level of activity and number of relationships.

These normal human dynamics require a change in leader relationships if the congregation is to grow. As the chart shows, around attendance of 100 the relationships become symmetrical. Now the pastor and the laity each expect to be in an equal relationship with each other. The type and location of congregational leadership shift. In churches of this size, the governing board, if there is one, becomes the significant locus of leadership. In the absence of a board, some kind of informal relationship will develop in which the pastor and the lay leaders carry out a dialogue regarding congregational decisions. The pastor's role is expected to be more that of initiator, less that of lover. She or he will have to spend more time developing programs, solving problems, and giving direction, and less time on the care and nurture of members. The congregation mourns that loss.

Because leadership is shared, the pastor's presence at board and committee meetings is more important than in churches with attendance of less than 100. Not only can the pastor initiate leadership, but decisions cannot "properly" be made unless both parties are present. Here is the primary obstacle to making the transition to the next larger size. As the congregation grows to about 200, the number of programs and relationships increases to the point that the pastor cannot be involved in every decision, and the management style is not decisive enough to handle this larger group.

The way symmetrical relationships are played out in congregations of this size varies. The pastor may be given the initiating prerogative in certain areas, the lay leader in others. The symmetry may be maintained by alternating the initiative according to some kind of implied reciprocal arrangement. Compromise often becomes the model for moving from disagreement to decision.

In order for a congregation to pass into the next size category—attendance of 200 and above—relationships must shift again to a complementary style, this time with the pastor one-up. The transition is usually marked by the employment of a second ordained or program staff person. The significance of this move in practical terms is to remove the senior member of the staff one level from the congregation. In some cases, a second staff person is placed in a symmetrical relationship with the first, which replaces the symmetrical relationship located up to that time between the pastor and the laity.

The decision-making characteristics in congregations of 200 or more therefore tend to emphasize the pastor's role. The larger the congregation grows beyond the 200 level, the clearer this emphasis becomes. The laity must then approach the pastor from a clear one-down position, and any hope for a lay leader to influence the direction of a congregation rests in his or her ability to influence the pastor.

The basic resistance in congregations to moving through these two attendance levels—100 and 200—comes from the need to change the pastor/laity relationships. This is the same kind of resistance frequently seen in families when adolescents try to negotiate a change in the relationship with their parents.

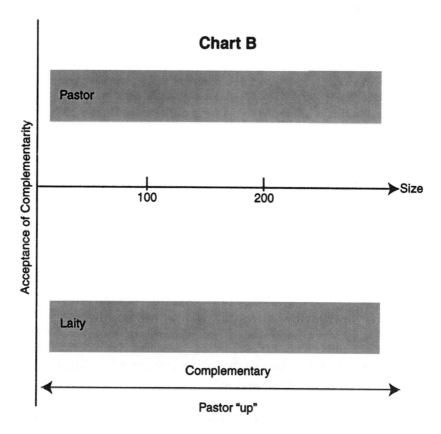

Some congregations move right through these levels with little difficulty or with no more than a temporary plateau in attendance. All large
churches at one time had attendance of less than 100 or fell in the 100-200
range. How this happens is illustrated in chart B. In this chart, the congregation and pastor begin with the assumption that the relationship between
pastor and laity is complementary, pastor one-up. In such a case the only
internal barrier to growth would lie in the pastor's lack of skill. People are
not likely to join such a congregation unless they are willing to accept the
power of the pastor. This is one possible reason why conservative churches
are growing. Conservative theology and social expectations are receptive
to a clearly stated authority figure, making larger congregations easier to
develop. This is demonstrated in the conservative fondness for very large
churches.

The nature of pastor/laity conflict is also influenced by the type of
leader relationships. In complementary relationships, the issue tends to be
personalized, for the self-understanding of each party is dependent upon the
existence of the other. In larger churches, the pastor is often personally
threatened by attempts of the laity to assume leadership prerogatives. The
reverse is true in the complementary relationships of churches with attendance of fewer than 100. At this level, the lay leaders are personally threatened by the pastor's attempts to challenge their one-up position. What
appears on the surface to be a disagreement about ideas is really a disagreement at the meta level, a conflict over relationships and power. The
only resolution in such situations is either for one of the two parties to back
off and accept the one-down position, or, if this is intolerable, to exit the
field.

Where symmetrical relationships are the norm, conflict often escalates
when each person is struggling to be equal to the other. The solution lies in
arbitration (sometimes difficult for congregations with a congregational polity to accept) or some kind of compromise.

It is important to recall two things as this paradigm is applied to congregations. One is that meta communications are always present, and they
tend to be subtle and nonverbal. A complicating factor is that there are
many complementary, pastor one-up, messages woven into church life. The
pulpit is raised, the pastor wears robes, the sermon is not a dialogue. Some
degree of complementarity is assumed.

The second thing is the question of propriety. Recall that "good" or
"bad" are not words that should be applied to these relationships. The question

is what is appropriate for the situation. A considerable degree of frustration and anger is generated when the expectations of the different parties do not match. A pastor who communicates a complementary–pastor one-up–relationship may be considered "bad" by congregational leaders who communicate in the reverse mode. Or a pastor who communicates a symmetrical relationship in a situation that calls for complementary–pastor one-up–relationships may be seen as weak or incompetent. These perceptions may be wrong but nonetheless affect the relationships.

NOTES

1. The numbers of 100 and 200 are approximate. The existence of plateaus in those ranges, however, is well attested through empirical evidence.

From Action Information *13, no. 4 (July/August 1987): pp. 1-5.*

CHAPTER 6

Beginnings of a Theory of Synagogue Size

Changing Patterns and Behaviors

Alice Mann, David Trietsch, and Dan Hotchkiss

The following scenarios might sound familiar:

• Temple Israel, founded by two families five years ago as an alternative to the large congregation across town, has grown to 67 families. At last spring's annual meeting there were two candidates for president. The election became unpleasant, and the oldest member of one founding family left the congregation.

• Beth El Synagogue has grown to three hundred families. This fall the board received a petition signed by a group that has been meeting in homes over the summer. The petition says the rabbi is too "cold and distant," pays too much attention to big donors and new members, and her contract should not be renewed.

• Temple Shaaray Tefila, which celebrated its 50th anniversary in January, has had about 450 members, give or take 20 or 30, for two decades. Its leaders wonder why the temple has not grown, despite three recruitment drives, a sound religious school, and the lowest dues of any temple in the city.

These scenarios echo patterns found in churches, patterns that have given rise to "church size theory," a body of experience and observations about how churches behave differently at different sizes and how they can get "stuck" at size transitions. But what would a synagogue-size theory look like? Exactly how do synagogues change as they grow and decline? What are the challenging transitions, and how can leaders help congregations to move through them successfully?

Nineteen synagogue consultants met in Boston in summer 2000 to explore these questions and others with Alban consultant Alice Mann, whose writings on church size have drawn attention in the Jewish world. In the top-floor conference room of the United Jewish Philanthropies building, Mann described the theory of church size most often used by the Alban Institute and drew on the experience of participants to learn how the ideas have already been adapted for use in synagogues. The group discussed the best way to measure synagogue size, the characteristics of synagogues of various sizes, and the challenges that transitional stages present in Jewish congregations.

After that workshop, the three of us (Mann, Trietsch, and Hotchkiss) met to consolidate what we learned and to clarify the questions stimulated by the encounter. When applying church-size concepts to the Jewish setting, it became clear to us that some generalizations useful to mainline Protestants need to be "relativized" in order to apply them to the different institutional realities in synagogues. A broader perspective will help consultants, including Alban consultants, to serve Jewish congregations. In the process, we hope to expand our understanding of congregation size in ways that will help us understand the full diversity of churches better, too.

Alban's approach to congregation size makes three basic assertions:

1. Congregations fall into distinctive size categories, and congregations of different sizes organize in different ways.
2. Congregations do not grow or decline smoothly, but tend to plateau at certain predictable sizes.
3. In order to successfully grow past a plateau, a congregation must deliberately break with familiar patterns of behavior and begin to act as larger congregations act.

At this conceptual level, the theory no doubt applies not only to synagogues, but to all institutions. It is well documented that humans tend to form primary groups of twelve or so and clans of about 50. At about 150, a qualitative shift (the "tipping point") occurs, and a true organization comes into being, with official roles and structures, overt communication, and formal procedures. Larger organizations generally seem to work best when built of combinations as these natural-sized groups.

These numbers underlie the specific size categories most often used by Alban in its work with churches. Developed by Arlin Rothauge, the categories are as follows:

Family-size church (up to 50 adults and children at worship). A small church organized around one or two matriarchs or patriarchs who often are the heads of extended biological families in the church. The pastor functions in a chaplain role, leading worship and giving pastoral care. A pastor who challenges the authority of a family-size church patriarch or matriarch or presumes to be the primary leader of the congregation generally will not stay long.

Pastoral-size church (50-150). The pastor is the central figure, holding together a small circle of leaders. Two or three major "fellowship groups" compose the congregation, but each member expects personal attention from the pastor. The pastor's time is largely taken up maintaining direct pastoral relationships with each member, coordinating the work of the leadership circle, and personally leading worship and small group programs, such as Bible study.

Program-size church (150-350). Known for the quality and variety of its programs. Separate programs for children, youth, couples, seniors, and other age and interest groups provide entry points for a wide range of people. The minister's role is to recruit, equip, and inspire a circle of key lay leaders and staff. Decision making is distributed, and pastoral care is shared by laity.

Corporate-size church (350 or more). Known for excellence in worship and music and for the range and diversity of its programs. Specialized ministries to narrowly identified groups of people, several of which aspire to be known beyond the congregation for their excellence. The senior pastor spends more time preparing to preach and lead worship than most clergy and must be skilled at working with a diverse staff of full-time professional leaders. A multi-layered structure of staff, boards, and committees perform the decision-making function. Clergy continue to provide pastoral care, especially in crisis moments, and most members find their spiritual support in small groups or from lay visitors.

In addition, the megachurches may require new categories ("resource churches" is one possibility) to describe new patterns of church.

The question, then, is, How do basic concepts of church size apply to the different norms and patterns of synagogue life? The question is complicated by the fact that synagogues vary a great deal. The Boston workshop, which drew consultants from various denominations of Judaism, has begun to define the questions that require research. In the remainder of this article, we will articulate these questions and offer our hunches and hypotheses about the answers.

What Is the Best Way to Measure Synagogue Size?

For churches, as noted above, average Sunday attendance, including both adults and children, generally is the best measure of size. Church membership statistics are notoriously unreliable, subject as they are to pastors' boasting and the accumulation of "dead wood." The number of pledging units is a second-best measure, as it includes only people who have taken action, but changes in this number tend to lag reality by two or three years. Also, pledging units may include either one or two adults. So attendance seems to be the best size measure for most purposes.

Synagogues customarily report their size as a number of family units. Because most congregations require annual dues payments, this figure is analogous to church pledging units, only perhaps a little firmer because a church pledge can be a token.

Worship attendance is less useful as a size marker for synagogues, which often have many dues-paying members who rarely attend regular worship services. Shabbat worship attendance is commonly as low as 10 to 40 percent of membership, especially in Reform and Conservative congregations. High spikes in the attendance graph frequently occur when a bar or bat mitzvah service is held during the Shabbat service. The High Holy Days are often the one time when almost all of the member attend services.

Sabbath worship attendance does not play the central binding role in most synagogues that it does in most churches. Other forms of participation, including sending children to religious school, Brotherhood or Sisterhood activity, home ritual observance, study group participation, and holding leadership positions may be regarded as equivalent indicators of active membership. There are exceptions: Orthodox congregations and the growing number of informal home minyans where Shabbat worship is more central. Workshop participants, however, reported a renewed emphasis on worship attendance as a central element of Jewish living.

The ways synagogues differ from churches call attention to some of the ways churches differ from each other. There are mainline Protestant churches where, temporarily at least, activities other than worship–Bible study, music groups, women's organizations, or committees–play the central role of binding members to the group. In Southern Baptist congregations, the kind of participation leaders track most carefully is Sunday school attendance (adults and children); while it is generally assumed that most will attend worship, church size and health are gauged by the Sunday school numbers. There are also new ways of organizing churches that divide the public "seekers service" from the smaller worship for believers; the seeker event seems more like an educational presentation or a rally than like traditional worship. The most common patterns of church life are not the only ones.

These observations suggest that, at least for synagogues (and perhaps for churches as well), there may be no one best measure of congregation size. The most useful measure probably depends on the question you are trying to answer.

If you want to know how many clergy and staff a congregation should hire, you need to understand the level of expectation for staff-intensive services such as religious school, adult education, and youth and young adult programs. In most synagogues, the most labor-intensive constituents are children up through bar or bat mitzvah age. A second group is older youth who remain active. A third is the active circle of adults who attend worship, call on the rabbis for pastoral care, and participate in adult study groups. The largest and least labor-intensive group is those who attend only occasionally and call on the synagogue only for weddings, memorial services, and other infrequent events.

If you want to know how large most members perceive the synagogue to be, then it will be important to look at the largest gatherings of members. Invariably this will include High Holy Days worship but may also include the annual fund-raising dinner or other events for which the entire congregation is expected.

If you want to describe the decision-making dynamics of the congregation, then you need to look for measures of the number who are active in synagogue governance. Possibilities include attendance at the annual meeting, size of the temple board, and participation in committees and affiliate groups. How many members would show up at a meeting to approve a new building? To select a rabbi? Such numbers can be no more than estimates, but it is important to have some idea how large a group may become involved, actually or potentially, in major synagogue decisions.

In future studies of synagogue size, we suggest the following tentative list of statistics that should be gathered, in approximate order of their systemic impact on the synagogue:

- number of children up to age 13 in member families who are enrolled in the synagogue religious school,

- number of children up to age 13 in member families who are enrolled in Jewish day schools,
- number of youth over 13 who participate in synagogue youth programs,
- number of adults who belong to member families,
- high Holy Days attendance,
- average Shabbat worship attendance.

It might be that with research and experience this list can be reduced to a simplified heuristic. But only by comparing all these measures (and perhaps others) with descriptions of the shape of congregational life can we define the typical size categories that will be most useful to leaders of synagogues.

AT WHAT SIZES DO SYNAGOGUES EXPERIENCE QUANTUM CHANGES IN THEIR MODE OF ORGANIZATION?

The easiest way to approach this question would be to ask experienced observers of synagogue life to identify congregations that they see as small, medium-sized, and large. Then those congregations could be studied using the size measures listed above.

This parallels and formalizes the way church-size theory was developed. Experts including Arlin Rothauge, Lyle Schaller, Carl George, and Gary McIntosh have proposed various size typologies for churches. These have intuitively made sense to other experienced observers, who in using them with congregants frequently hear, "This clarifies so much in our church that has been puzzling!" Formal research has been scarce, partly because the size-category idea has seemed so self-evidently true and useful.

Data are not completely absent. Various denominational bodies have reported from time to time on the distribution of their congregations by attendance or membership—more could be learned from such in-house statistics. Mark Chavez has constructed an unusually large congregational database in the National Congregations Study—an interesting finding about the correlation between size and worship has already been reported in the brief volume *How Do We Worship*, whetting the appetite for further exploration of the NCS data. New quantitative research about size and size transition will have to grapple more fully with a theoretical question: how does size interrelate with other variables as we try to describe differences among congregations? Organizational theorists Danny Miller and Peter Friesen argue for empirically derived "configurations" based on the way multiple variables most frequently coincide. A review of all the major congregational typologies developed in the past 30 years—and an identification of the variables each framework takes into account—would be a helpful resource.

The wish to adapt congregation-size theory to the synagogue supplies further impetus to study congregation size—in churches, synagogues, and other congregations—with more rigor. We began this process in a very small way at the Boston workshop with two case studies that suggest, as much by their deficiencies as by their merits, how such research might look.

The first case study was of an exceptionally fast-growing Reform temple in a suburb west of Boston. Aided by a growing Jewish population, the congregation experienced almost unbroken growth from its founding in 1963. The closest thing to a plateau in this synagogue's story came in 1973-75, when the curve hesitated at 150 member families. The temple history explains this hesitation as a result of a conflict over the rabbi, and sure enough, the growth resumed almost immediately after the rabbi left. In 1996 the temple implemented a membership cap at 450. With the retirement of the long-tenured rabbi who favored the cap, it remains to be seen how long it will be retained and how a congregation that has known only growth will deal with a self-imposed plateau.

Case Study #1

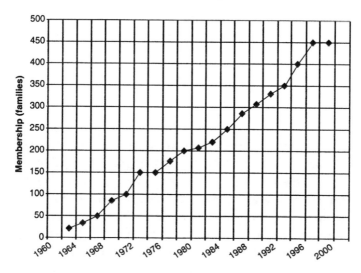

This example offers little evidence to support the idea of size plateaus where congregations tend to get stuck. Is this generally true of synagogues? Would the picture change if measures of size other than family membership were used? Only further studies can shed light on these questions.

The second case presented at the workshop was from a Boston congregation whose neighborhood has not experienced growth in either the general or the Jewish population. In 1986, the rabbi retired after 28 years, which may explain the loss of membership over the next five years. From 1987-94, the congregation employed a rabbi who in1992 asked that his salary and duties be reduced. In 1995 a new rabbi arrived who reopened the religious school and, after two years, was increased to full-time status.

Case Study #2

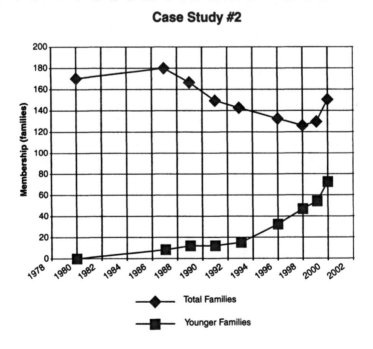

This case follows a pattern familiar to observers of the declining urban "Old First Church." In the 1980s, this synagogue plateaued at about 170 families; through the 1990s, it declined to a low of about 130 families. But over the same two decades there has been a steady and accelerating increase in the proportion of families with children. The membership records distinguish between "older" and "younger" families, with the latter group presumably providing most of the children for the religious school.

The synagogue had no younger families in 1980, but by 2000 almost half the families were younger.

Many questions remain unanswered by this glimpse of congregational history. Would the same pattern of growth and decline appear if we used different measures of congregational size? What are the mechanisms that retard growth in the face of an influx of young families? Is it simply that the older generation has died off, or would organizational changes have to occur in order to grow past the plateau?

It would be useful to have a description of the congregation's program, formal and informal structure, and the role of the rabbi and other leaders. With a number of such descriptions, plus various measures of size, we could discover the points of size transition and a generalized description of the traits of synagogues within each category. With this information, consultants, clergy, and lay leaders could help congregations to make sense of what is happening and to see what needs to change in order to become effective at each size.

CONCLUSION

Churches and synagogues are different in many ways, and yet like all organizations they shift to new patterns of organization and behavior as they grow and decline. Some leaders and observers of synagogue life have accepted this idea and have adapted and translated congregation-size theory and have applied it to synagogue life. For example, the consultants from the Boston workshop were able to substantiate from their experience in congregations that as congregational communities shifted from one size category to anothe, the three characteristics observed in churches hold true. First, the expectations of congregants change. Second, the roles of the rabbi, professional staff, and lay leadership are redefined, and third, the infrastructure—number of staff, ways to communicate, and so forth—needed to support the organization changes.

In the dialog begun at the Boston workshop, we began to clarify the questions that need to be answered in order to develop a size theory that is tailored to Jewish institutions, not adapted to them from elsewhere. In the process, we expect to gain insights that will be of help across the full spectrum of diversity in congregational life.

Part Two

The Ups and Downs of Congregational Size

CHAPTER 7

Growing Pains

Are They Worth It?

Bill Joiner

W hen asked if they want their church to grow, most church members reply, "Well, of course!" It seems to be a general assumption that growth means that the church will simply get bigger and that little will be different. It is a false assumption. People who want their churches to grow seldom give much thought to the fact that growing churches always change—the greater the growth, the more radical the change.

A better question might be, do you want growth knowing that growth will mean change?

The following is a story of how one congregation decided to test itself about its willingness to pay the price for growth. This congregation is twelve years old and is located in a suburb of Kansas City. Its growth seems to have stopped at an average Sunday worship attendance of 130 people. For these twelve years, the church has been a pastoral-size congregation. Many of the members want to grow into a program-size church.

In order to help the congregation assess its willingness to change (that is, its readiness to grow), I proposed a workshop, which was scheduled for a Sunday afternoon. The purpose of the workshop was to help the people of the church grapple with their feelings about growth and change.

The pastor put the question succinctly in his vision for the church: Do we want to be a mall or a country store? A characteristic of malls, he suggested, is anchor stores, those large department stores that give stability to the mall as a corporation. He spoke of staff people as anchors for the church. If it is decided that this church is to have significant growth, other anchors, namely, someone to be in charge of new member assimilation, will be needed soon.

Next, we divided into five discussion groups of about six people each. Three questions guided the discussions:

1. What changes are anticipated if our church grows significantly?
2. Will church growth seriously change our mission?
3. What would our church be like without significant growth?

ANTICIPATED CHANGES

When considering the first question, people generally agreed that significant growth would mean significant change. There would be changes in the church structure. Communications would need to be improved. One group especially emphasized the importance of communication in the planning process if the church were larger. This growth would inevitably mean more staff. The congregation also felt that growth would mean change in the style of leadership, and the pastor would become more of an administrator. There would also be a need for a greater number of volunteers in the church to keep programs functioning. One group felt that some of the friendliness of a small church would be lost and recommended an intentional effort to keep the church a place where people could find friendship and support.

Members suggested certain specifics needed to accommodate a larger church: more parking, more income, and more space (some felt this meant a new sanctuary). One person with a positive outlook concluded that if the facilities expanded, there would be less grass to mow.

CHANGES IN CHURCH PURPOSE

The second question was whether significant church growth would necessitate significant change in the way the church perceived its purpose. One group suggested not only that change was the price of growth, but that the church needed change and that the change should include a new vision and new goals. Another group was adamant that there should be no change in the mission of the church. They thought that the "guiding philosophy" had served the church well during its history and that it should continue to be the touchstone for decisions, plans, and goals.

Another group believed that while the essential purpose would not change, there would be a different emphasis. New members would bring new ideas, and this group thought that these new ideas should be intentionally solicited and welcomed. The church would also need to convert more members into ministers. One group said the changing purpose would include broadening the mission of the church. One group thought that the church would be more exciting and thus become a more vibrant congregation that would attract more interest and have higher expectations of itself.

If one purpose of the church is to be a family, the congregation recognized that they would need to develop small groups in which a family atmosphere could be continued.

A CHURCH WITH NO GROWTH

The third question asked people to project what life would be like for this church if no significant growth happened within the next five years. (Significant growth would mean that the church grew beyond its current membership. Obviously, any church has to replace members who, for whatever reason, are no longer members of the church. In a very mobile community churches have to work hard to replace those who move away. Significant growth however, is not simply replacing members, but growing into a different sized church. It had been suggested by the pastor that this would mean growing beyond an average Sunday attendance of 200.)

Some people believed that church members would become discouraged and, perhaps, burned out in their efforts to help the church grow. Others suggested that the church would have to adjust to whatever size it may be and carry on its work. Some thought that, if the church does not grow in membership, it could focus on individual spiritual growth and work toward quality programming within the church.

Generally, most people indicated that growth was crucial to the church and that no growth would have serious negative consequences for the church. Members suggested that some people would not be interested in a "country store" type of church. The implication was that the "general store" is out of character with their suburban community. Two of the groups thought that lack of growth would mean that the pastor would probably leave.

People expressed the opinion that much of the dream that has powered the church for its twelve-year history would be in jeopardy. The prospects for a new sanctuary would be lost. Programs would be limited. The music program would suffer, and families and youth would not find the church attractive. One group could see nothing positive in the failure to grow, and their negative list included:

• stagnation within the church,
• loss of leadership, and
• burnout among church workers.

Finally, some people believed that lack of growth would indicate a failure to live up to God's mandate for their church.

Members of one group thought that they would become an aging church. ("Rocking chairs might replace pews," one participant suggested.) Some suggested that not only would the congregation become an aging church, but aging buildings would have higher maintenance needs. This group concluded that lack of growth would mean waste of potential, pastoral leadership, real estate, and talent.

Conclusions and Recommendations

Approximately 35 people participated in the workshop, a little more than 25 percent of the worshipping congregation. The question could be asked: So how do the other 75 percent of the congregation feel about changes, about the purpose of the church, and about what would result from a no-growth situation at their church? The question is important. However, it could be argued that those who were at the workshop are the "movers and shakers" of the congregation. This group carries out much of the ministry of the church. They are the planners and goal setters. They are the people who coordinate ministries and oversee the programs, and they are the people who will make a church growth program work.

Workshop participants were aware that growth would have its cost in the life of the congregation, that to grow significantly would bring new ideas and, perhaps, new norms. But they were convinced that the alternative to growth is not acceptable. As one group emphasized, "There has been enough talk. Just do it!"

I offered the following suggestions at this just-do-it point in the life of this congregation:

1. Determine what size you want to be. Learn the dynamics of that size church and start living that way. If you want to be a program-size church (150-250 attendance in church on Sunday), make programming a priority over pastoral care, and free up the pastor to emphasize program

planning and implementation. Find ways to involve the congregation in pastoral care. (Actually, this congregation is already involved in training its laity to do crisis ministry.)

2. Make programming reflect your understanding of the needs of the people you want to attract to your church. One possibility is to study a church that you consider to be programming successfully for the community. What programs are you best prepared to offer, given the experience and interests of the people in your congregation? Prioritize the possibilities and go for the most important.

3. Bring on board your second staff person, "the assimilator" (the congregation's name for this new staff position). It would be important to be very clear about what is expected of this person, what qualifications he or she should have, and how "the assimilator" will work with the existing staff and church structure.

4. Contract for a training event for people in your church who are responsible for church growth. Help them learn how people go through stages of assimilation into the life and mission of a church. Explore ways to plan programming around these stages.

5. Cultivate an attitude of adventure within the congregation. The journey will be risky and exciting. If people catch the spirit of excitement and expectation, the church will be well on its way toward an expanded ministry within its community.

Put in organizational development terms, such changes as this congregation is contemplating will change its culture, its self-concept, its atmosphere, and its inner relationships. It is a difficult change to bring about, but not impossible. "To speak about organization change is well and good, but the fact is that it is much more difficult to bring about than individual change . . . . The incentive, of course, is that the payout is much greater. True organization development is a systemwide approach to change aimed at improving the 'whole' organization."[1]

As churches test their incentives to grow, they learn the price and determine whether the changes growth will bring have the right "payout" for them and their mission.

NOTES

1. Robert R. Blake and Anne Adams McCanse, *Leadership Dilemmas—Grid Solutions* (Houston: Gulf Publishing Company, 1991).

This article originally appeared in Congregations: The Alban Journal *14, no. 1 (January/February 1993): pp.3-5.*

CHAPTER 8

Raising the Roof

Foundations for the Breakthrough to Program Size

Alice Mann

Five years ago, a prestigious Boston medical school started to "raise the roof"—to build a brand new seventh floor atop an older, six-story building. Construction was well under way before the architects discovered, to their horror, that the existing structure was not strong enough to carry the weight of the new addition. Project leaders had to make a costly and embarrassing trip back to the drawing board.

In June and July 2000, I studied the experience of seven congregations—all United Church of Christ churches in southeastern Massachusetts—moving through the transition zone between pastoral and program size. While their stories are complex and contain much that is particular to their specific situations, these congregations have helped me to understand what it might mean to "lay the foundation" for a difficult size transition. In this chapter, I will discuss four preparatory tasks that might keep a church—especially a mainline Protestant congregation in a growing community—from suffering the same fate as our Boston architects:

- excavating the religious culture(s) of their congregation,
- building a foundation for change using the congregation's own cultural materials,
- enriching the congregation's practices of democracy and discernment,
- assessing the congregation's progress on key dimensions of system change.

When the groundwork has been laid in these four ways, "raising the roof"—that is, expanding institutional capacity in order to meet community opportunities and needs—becomes a realizable dream.

Assumptions behind the Research

I began my research with one major assumption, namely, that a vital congregation searches for ways to reach and serve its surrounding population. Faith communities vary dramatically, of course, in the way they define the terms "reach," "serve," and "surrounding population." But for me, this is a foundational premise that branches into several corollaries.

First, I assume that growth in average Sabbath attendance is one (but not the only) relevant measure of how adequately a congregation meets the needs of a growing community. (All of the study churches were located in growing towns, and the findings of this research are especially applicable to congregations facing the opportunities and challenges presented by population growth.)

Second, I assume that planting a new congregation is one effective way to reach a growing population; in that case, most of the growth in attendance takes place in the newly formed congregation. Changing size—"stepping up" decisively to a new level of institutional capacity—is another way to address the opportunity of population growth.

Third, I assume that size change, and especially the shift from pastoral to program size, is one of the most difficult transitions a congregation will ever navigate. Many aspects of the congregation's culture will have to change, and the church's enduring values will have to be expressed in new ways if the shift is to be made successfully.

Finally, I assume that size affects a congregation's public role. Community organizers have noted that larger congregations make better institutional partners for neighborhood improvement. Family- and pastoral-size churches have greater difficulty establishing human service programs, securing grants, forming community development corporations, and engaging in advocacy on behalf of vulnerable populations. Short-tenured and part-time pastors (common in churches with average attendance under 100) have less opportunity to develop community relationships or assume leadership positions within local boards and organizations.

Against this conceptual backdrop, let us look at what is involved in laying the groundwork for a pastoral- to program-size transition.

PREPARATORY TASK 1
EXCAVATING THE RELIGIOUS CULTURE(S) OF THE CONGREGATION

"Excavating the religious culture" sounds a bit like archaeology. A fine new resource called *How We Seek God Together: Exploring Worship Style*[1] makes the case for viewing congregations as distinctive cultures. The authors define congregational cultures as "tool kits" made up of "stories, symbols, rituals, patterns of thought, world views with which people build a way of life." A congregation's culture (or cultures, because more than one distinctive culture may be manifest within a single congregation) can be explored by studying various cultural products—such as worship, buildings or other physical artifacts, and mission activity in the local context.

Congregations with different cultures will define a term like "mission to the surrounding community" in different ways and will assign different religious meanings to an apparent opportunity for numerical growth. Using categories developed by church sociologists Carl Dudley, William McKinney, and Jackson Carroll in *Varieties of Religious Presence*[2] we might characterize these different stances toward growth in broad terms.

For congregations with an *activist* religious culture, "God calls the *congregation* to speak out on issues and engage in corporate action, working for social change...." Some activist churches see no need to be more than small cadres, more concerned about commitment than numbers; others seek to "build their base" of ministry (and consequently their numbers) through community organizing techniques.

Congregations with a *civic* culture promote the public good through involvement with existing social and economic institutions. Internally, a congregation of this type "provides a forum in which social issues can be discussed and debated in a way that enables *individual* members to act responsibly as Christians...." Civic churches tend to see themselves as part of the community fabric. They may view Sabbath attendance as a minor measure as compared to the total number of people whose lives are touched by the ministries of the congregation and by the leavening influence of members scattered throughout the community. On the other hand, they may see building membership as a way to foster strength, openness, and diversity in their "little public." (I will elaborate on this last point in my discussion of task 3.)

In a more *evangelistic* church culture, the "spirit of the Great Commission is at the center of congregational life," and congregants are "encouraged to witness to their faith, sharing the message of salvation with those outside the fellowship...." Generally speaking, this religious tradition tends to value numerical growth as a sign that the Good News is being proclaimed effectively and that more people are being called into a life of discipleship. Numerical aspirations may be affected, however, by the degree of theological conformity required of new members.

Where the congregation sees itself primarily as *sanctuary*, members are called across the threshold into the congregation to experience divine transcendence over the trials of daily life. Christians are "expected to live in the world, accepting it as it is, and to uphold its laws; but they are to be 'not of this world' in their deepest loyalty which belongs only to God." Because weekly worship is a key spiritual discipline, growing attendance may be seen as an indicator that the congregation is engaged in effective spiritual formation of its members and inquirers. On the other hand, members may understand themselves as the "faithful remnant" and may expect few others to join them as they seek to enter through the narrow gate.

These four congregational cultures are "tool kits"[3] available to faith communities as they interpret shifts in their context and re-imagine their own role in a changed environment. *How We Seek God Together* is an excellent guide for exploring the culture of your faith community in order to lay the groundwork for a size transition.

"GOLDEN RULE" CHRISTIANITY

No single set of categories can adequately describe all the nuances of congregational culture. Recent work by church sociologist Nancy Ammerman in "Spiritual Journeys in the American Mainstream"[4] offers another perspective on cultural differences that helped me to understand the seven churches in the study—as well as other congregations I have worked with on issues of numerical growth. Her analysis of extensive data from 23 churches (ranging from fundamentalist to Unitarian) revealed that about half the members overall shared an approach to religious life that she termed "Golden Rule" Christianity. This group was at least a substantial minority in even the most conservative congregations. Her appreciative portrayal of this cultural subgroup found within a wide spectrum of congregations may help you to interpret some of the growth-related conversations (and silences) in your own church.

Based on Ammerman's interviews, here are the kinds of phrases an imaginary group of Golden Rule Christians might use to describe their own spiritual path:

- The most important attributes of a Christian are caring for the needy and living one's Christian values every day.
- The most important task of the church is service to people in need.
- The Bible is important (even though few of us would call it the "inerrant" word of God).
- We are less concerned with answering life's great questions or developing a rigorous theological system than with practices that cohere into something we can call a "good life."
- Our goal is neither to change another person's beliefs nor to change the whole political system. We would like the world to be a bit better for our having inhabited it.
- We have not given up on transcendence. The church's "sacred space" and the "sacred time" set aside for worship give many of us an opportunity to set our priorities in order, "feed the soul," and know that we have been in a presence greater than ourselves.

Most of the leaders I met in the course of my study expressed their faith using a Golden Rule idiom.[5]

If Ammerman's findings were shown to be representative of the general population, Golden Rule Christians would constitute the largest subset of church members in the United States. This possibility could help explain why so many congregations have difficulty with the topic of numerical growth. Since Golden Rule Christians place a very high value on diversity and tolerance, they are not eager to challenge other people's religious beliefs or even, in most situations, to verbalize their own. One woman wrote me a letter explaining her feelings.

When I visited my grandparents in a small northern New York State town as a child of seven, I was reprimanded for going down by the railroad tracks with my friend to try to peek at those "strange people" who set up a tent to shout out the glory of God, sing boisterous hymns, and pray .... I don't think that this [association with the religious culture of "holy rollers"] was an unusual social stigma. Those of my age now ... sometimes find it difficult to

speak publicly about our faith and so we dedicate ourselves to the
work of God and His Church. Doesn't the Church grow in spite of
that type of faith?

Golden Rule Christians often exhibit an appealing modesty about their faith.
Where this reticence is more intense, however, leaders may vehemently
reject invitational outreach of any kind—even gentle communication with
people who share (or who would readily appreciate) the congregation's
approach to faith. This "allergic" reaction stands in tension with other core
values of the Golden Rule path, such as offering a caring welcome for
newcomers in the community. Though American culture in the 1950s oper-
ated like a dump truck, depositing people at the church's front door on
Sunday morning so that mainline Protestant Christians could greet them, it
now whisks prospective members off to the mall, the soccer field, the office, or the weekend getaway. Congregations that want to show "hospitality
to the stranger" may need to build a more visible path (metaphorically and
literally) to the doors of their spiritual home and provide more explanation
about their faith tradition for those who do appear on the doorstep. But the
"allergy" must be addressed in order for this kind of outreach to occur.

Across the sample of churches in the study, a number of specific issues
emerged that related to the prominence of Golden Rule Christianity within
each congregation's cultural makeup.

Intending growth. Congregations with a Golden Rule religious culture have
an especially hard time forming, expressing, or endorsing an intention to
grow numerically. Though all seven churches I studied were located in
growing towns and were visited regularly by newcomers, many leaders
disavowed any goal to increase church attendance. When my questions
included the word "growth," interviewees often prefaced their answers
with a definition of the term that did not involve an increase in numbers. The
subject seemed to provoke more than intellectual disagreement; in many
conversations, the idea of explicitly *seeking growth* seemed to provoke
slight twinges of discomfort, embarrassment, or distaste. Growth that "just
happens" may be acceptable (and even a source of quiet satisfaction for
some), but numerical growth intentionally sought seemed somehow to be
regarded as an unworthy or shameful goal.

Only a few of the leaders I interviewed volunteered a clear moral
or theological case for stepping up to the next size in order to make
room for the people moving into their communities. In several of these

congregations, leaders were surprised to see that their worship attendance had been stuck at a plateau for several years; tracking attendance trends was not part of their annual self-assessment.

Emphasis on children. With an apparent preponderance of Golden Rule Christians in the pews, what motivated the seven churches I studied to work at the tasks required for a size transition? By and large, concern for children and their parents was the biggest driving factor that pressed these congregations to expand their capacity—even in the face of their reluctance to embrace numerical growth as an overall goal. "Religious and moral training for their children," says Ammerman, is "central in the circle of care" that defines a virtuous life for Golden Rule Christians. Within the seven churches in the "Raising the Roof" study, the Christian education committee typically played a key role in advocating for growth plans. Dynamic younger women often led the charge, and a few of these gifted leaders were later selected to serve as paid Christian education staff. In one of the churches, the elder generation placed a high value on reaching children even before younger families had arrived in any number. Their long-range plan called bluntly for a transition to a new generation.

Children in worship. In the churches I studied, parents tended to want their children with them in worship at least part of the time each week. Children typically attended the first part of the service and participated in communion when it was offered; one church went further by creating a new "early service" that involves children throughout. For some of the empty-nest and elder adults in these churches, weekly connection with youngsters in worship was a joy. For others (and even, perhaps, for some younger parents), this practice seemed to collide with a longing for transcendence, which they may have had a hard time articulating. Ammerman's work sheds light on these particular yearnings. When she asked Golden Rule Christians about their experience of God, they often paused to search for words; some then responded that they felt "close to God in Sunday worship, especially in the music and in the opportunity for quiet reflection." Because Golden Rule members are less likely than others to attend programs designed for adult spiritual formation, especially in small group settings, many of these adults may cling to those familiar worship patterns as their one reliable touchstone with transcendence. This group may feel bereft of their particular experience of the holy when worship becomes more focused on children (one argument for multiple worship services).

Spiritual growth. By understanding and respecting the congregation's existing culture(s), leaders may develop the trust required to guide each cultural group–including the Golden Rule Christians–toward appropriate forms of spiritual growth. Religious cultures are dynamic; they evolve over time in response to external circumstances, internal needs, and the overtures of individual leaders. Ammerman challenges congregations to help Golden Rule adults and their children to develop a "sustained religious vocabulary" and to "[build] up the store of moral resources on which they can call for living the good and caring life to which they say they aspire." She concludes that the spiritual yearnings of the Golden Rule group are "as real as they are vague" and deserve respectful attention. The difficulty comes in persuading these members that they should actually show up for experiences that would deepen their spiritual life–especially in small groups.

Among the seven churches I studied, one had a particularly effective strategy for adult education and spiritual development that seemed to fulfill Ammerman's challenge with considerable success. Headed by a volunteer director (a retired private school dean), this program included twenty different adult faith development offerings in the course of the year. Some were clergy led, but most were not. Some lasted three or four sessions, while others were long-term study groups. The overall menu of choices addressed different styles of spirituality and learning.

It is probably not a coincidence that this same congregation scored especially high on two measures used in the study. The first instrument–developed in the course of this research–is the "System Change Index," which locates a congregation on nine dimensions of organizational transition required for healthy functioning at program size. (See appendix A for a list of these dimensions.) This particular church received the highest possible rating on almost every dimension. Its adult education strategy was just one example of its consistently "program" way of doing things–a variety of choices, high quality, and the deployment of staff (in this case, a talented volunteer) to organize and direct a program delivered by many different leaders.

The second instrument was the "Margin in Life" inventory, developed by nursing researcher Joanne Stevenson.[6] This inventory measures the impact of various factors, including religious practice, on a person's available reserves of energy, vitality, and resilience–a surplus she calls "margin." Adults draw upon these reserves when they embrace an opportunity for personal growth and learning, or when they confront a challenge such as illness, grief, or unexpected change. (See Appendix B for a list of the factors measured by the "Margin-in-Life" instrument.) I administered this inventory to about thirty people in each church. Members of the particular congregation I have been describing seemed to have more "margin" in their daily lives; on average, these congregants scored highest among the seven congregations. Although this finding caught my attention, the variations in average "margin" scores might well have arisen from demographic differences among towns and congregations rather than from differences in church structure or programming. But the specific contribution of religion to a member's "margin in life" was also the highest in this particular church. It seems reasonable to speculate that differences in scores on the religion factor might indicate a real difference in the impact each congregation makes on its members. Because my study involved such a small sample of congregations, this finding is only suggestive, but it reinforces a strong hunch. Remaining stuck in the transition zone seems to drain the margin (personal reserves of energy, vitality, and resilience) out of leaders and active members. Full transition to a "program" way of operating—combined with explicit attention to the spiritual development of adults—seems to allow a congregation to enhance people's "margin in life" more effectively.

PREPARATORY TASK 2
BUILDING A FOUNDATION FOR CHANGE
USING THE CONGREGATION'S OWN CULTURAL MATERIALS

When addressing growth opportunities, mainline Protestant congregations proceed from their own understandings of religious authority. Neither a Bible verse nor an admonition from the hierarchy will automatically answer to members' satisfaction the question: "Should we grow?" Resources from the church growth movement sometimes emphasize understandings of scriptural and pastoral authority that are foreign to—or constitute a minority position within—the religious culture of mainline Protestant churches. It seems that congregations with a liberal theology and a democratic polity need to "construct" the authority to change size from materials already available within their own religious culture. Some of these "materials" (potential cultural resources for authorizing a size change) may be well developed and ready at hand; the Golden Rule value on ministering to children and families is an example of a well-developed cultural resource for authorizing certain kinds of growth. Other cultural materials needed for constructing this foundation may currently lie out of reach, buried in one of two forms. They may lie underground as cultural "ore"–latent source materials never uncovered or processed at all. (Each member's own faith story, for example, is a latent resource that, if brought to awareness and articulation, could provide people with the inner authority to invite others in authentic and respectful ways.) On the other hand, these cultural resources may lie beneath the surface in the form of "lost treasure"–developed cultural materials discarded at a certain point in history or entombed in layers of cultural accretion. (An example of "lost treasure" might be the pre-Reformation spiritual traditions that shaped the faith of Luther and Calvin but were not carried forward into the next generation of Protestant religious life.) Constructing a foundation of authority for size change from materials that already belong to the religious culture may be an arduous task; nevertheless, this seems the surest way to build a solid basis for growth efforts.

For an individual leader, the issue of authority presents itself as a very practical question: "What right do I have to ask others in this church to change?" Or perhaps more pointedly, "What right do I have to ask this congregation to relinquish some of its familiar patterns and to adopt some new ways of being church?" Much has been written about the way an effective pastor brings personal authority (trustworthiness tested in the crucible of relationship) to his or her position of organizational power. Pastor and author James Adams[7] has captured this central challenge of clergy leadership in a single question: "Do I want to be in control or do I want to be taken seriously?" If the pastor is seen as being disrespectful of the congregation's culture (perhaps by disparaging the congregation's favorite hymns and instructing the musician to substitute "better" choices, for example), a power struggle will probably ensue. Members will feel that they have to defend the congregation's way of life against the intruder; in a process with many unconscious dimensions, the ruling spirit of the church's culture will "knight" certain people to do battle on its behalf. In contrast, when clergy proceed from an attitude of cross-cultural curiosity and respect, resistance to change is generally less severe. The way clergy exercise their religious authority does indeed have a major impact on the way a change is received.

However, when it comes to making a major shift with big implications for the church's culture–like the pastoral- to program-size transition–the authority of lay leaders becomes pivotal. By lay leaders, I mean not only the formal officeholders, but also the informal opinion leaders within various constituencies. Even more than pastors, laypeople receive "permission" to lead to the extent that they are recognized (at least subconsciously) as carriers of the church's culture. This is particularly true in family- and pastoral-size congregations, where the dominant style is easily perceived and conserved. But even in larger congregations, where some cultural variety is likely to be acknowledged and negotiated, the most influential leaders are probably those who embody (or defer to) the dominant culture.

If a lay leader makes a bid to modify that culture (in response to new realities in the environment or new needs among members), he or she must demonstrate that the proposed change is "authorized" by values at the center of the culture itself. The change will only occur if it comes to be viewed as a "natural" step, a new chapter that emerges coherently from a unique congregational narrative. Except where there is a very long-tenured and well loved pastor, lay leaders may actually have more authority than clergy to initiate cultural change, provided that they are astute interpreters of the congregation's story and have a clear "read" on the external environment. Perhaps you can see why I chose to place "excavating the religious culture(s) of the congregation" first on the list of preparatory tasks. A handful of well-trusted members can lead the way as the faith community retraces its roots and reinterprets its central values for a new day.

We turn now to some of the specific clues about sources of authority that surfaced in the study churches.

Biblical Authority

When asked directly, the pastor(s) and two lay leaders I interviewed in each church agreed rather strongly with the general assertion that growth is a biblical mandate. But in six of the seven churches, lay leaders almost never used biblical language or mentioned biblical themes when they talked about growth in their individual interviews or in the group story telling. In only one church did a lay leader volunteer a statement that it was God's or Jesus' will that the church should grow at this time. Ammerman notes that a disinclination to invoke the Bible in an explicit or literalistic way does not mean that Golden Rule Christians find the Bible unimportant. In many cases, they simply have little practice putting into their own words the faith that underlies their everyday actions. Baby boomers with this faith style also tend to forget that they grew up in an environment saturated with religious stories and symbols. Although they may be able to draw on this spiritual capital in times of need or decision, they may overlook the need to replenish that capital for themselves or to help succeeding generations understand the spiritual root system that generated the Golden Rule branch of religious life. (Paradoxically, notes Ammerman, they often undercut their own hopes for their children by neglecting the transmission of basic stories and precepts.) So, except for one church—whose culture includes both evangelical and Golden Rule components—the Bible was a tacit, but not an explicit, source of authority for size change in the congregations I studied.

Pastoral Authority

The lay leaders that I interviewed generally agreed with the assertion that their pastors "believe the church should grow at this time." But they often emphasized that the pastor's organizational role in promoting size change was low-key or behind the scenes—helping the congregation move toward its own decisions. Low-key did not mean insignificant; lay leaders noted the quiet power of their pastors' leadership. All seven clergy showed a marked preference for the "supporting" style of leadership (measured by the Blanchard LBA II inventory[8]) as opposed to a style of directing, coaching, or delegating. Several of the clergy manifested some ambivalence about seeking (or even tracking) growth in worship attendance. Despite their desire for growth in program scope, quality, and inclusiveness, this subset of the pastors seemed to mirror their congregations' hesitance to work explicitly toward increasing the average worship attendance (which I take to be one relevant measure of the congregation's caring for the spiritual needs of a growing town).

Golden Rule Authority

The Christian education leaders in each congregation who argued for expanded capacity—to serve children and their families better—were building a foundation for growth from materials already available in the church's religious culture. Although any of the seven churches could probably serve as a case to illustrate this point, I will provide sample cultural materials from just one of the congregations.

- A report of the Christian Education Committee to the Annual Meeting in 1959 began with this statement about the committee's work: "We know that unless we are a teaching church, we are not a true church, so our greatest emphasis is on our Church School."
- The second sentence of the mission statement adopted by this church in 1996 reads: "Seeking God's guidance we aim, through the effective use of our resources, to meet present-day challenges, especially the fellowship, parenting, and Christian education needs of our congregation."
- Early in 1999, an "elder statesman" of this church looked back over the previous ten years in the address he gave on Appreciation Sunday. "During the early and mid-eighties at virtually all Church Council Meetings, three real 'Needs' developed. The *first* and most serious need was the problem of not enough space or rooms for our Sunday school classes. Ellie Noyes, who then, as now, primarily engineered this program, would plead, 'Where can I have my classes?' and indeed there was no good answer."

The power to authorize change does not lie in the documents themselves—current leaders may not recall or refer to these particular statements. The power lies in the underlying values of this congregation's religious culture, which are expressed in a variety of ways. Through the years, leaders in this church have showed confidence that they could legitimately ask their fellow members for change, sacrifice, and institutional expansion—provided that the purpose was religious education for children.

Leaders in the seven churches have generally shown far less confidence about asking for change when the purpose is to increase (or, to put it more delicately, allow natural growth in) overall attendance. From a Golden Rule perspective, this is a tougher case to make. Nevertheless, one lay leader I interviewed did articulate an unusually passionate, Golden Rule case for stepping up to the next size:

Ultimately, the message we kept trying to put out was Christian responsibility—not only to ourselves—responsibility to everyone who chooses to be part of us. If people want to worship here, we have a responsibility to furnish a second service, [second] Sunday school—[enough] programs to allow them to participate. This touches the consciences of people, and I have no conscience [i.e., qualms] about playing on people's consciences! Many are

in between: "I want growth but...." There are things I'm not all
that crazy about that are part of going from a small to a larger
church—people I hardly ever see, not knowing too many on Sunday, though they know me. There is no free lunch.

This leader is one of the many early-retirees who have moved to southeastern Massachusetts in the past decade. Based on his intense volunteer involvement with affordable housing advocacy, I would say that he personally
manifests more of an activist than a Golden Rule religious culture. But by
framing the question of growth in terms of "Christian responsibility," he was
speaking a language that Golden Rule Christians would tend to take seriously. What most surprised his fellow members may have been his passion
about issues of growth, but his quiet one-to-one approach helped others to
grapple with his message.

Another respected leader of this congregation (a woman recovering
from recent breast cancer who had been part of this church for more than
twenty years) described the impact of his witness on her own and others'
thinking. "[He provided a] tremendous push. He exemplifies what true Christianity is . . . very quiet [but still saying to us], 'This is what the Gospel is all
about.' I thought, 'Oh, yeah! How could I have thought differently?'" As
opposition to growth began to manifest itself, those who favored expansion
began to take a more conscious stand. "[We asked ourselves] 'What is our
message?' Spread the word! Include children! Evangelistic work, open doors,
invite, grow! Once I was 'there' I was happy—this is what I really believe.
That was an 'Aha!' experience." In the middle of a tense and crucial meeting, she testified to the powerful support this congregation had provided
during her cancer treatment, and she laid down a spiritual challenge: "I
don't want this church divided." Others told her later that her speech had
"turned them around." A large majority of those at the meeting endorsed
the growth-related initiatives (including the two-service schedule already in
place).

It appears that the newer leader—an assertive cultural "outsider" with
activist inclinations—was able to awaken the conscience of Golden Rule
members about their responsibility to make room for newcomers. Though
he himself may not have used evangelical language, he seems to have stirred
up in others some previously unexpressed convictions about spreading the
Gospel. Although this advocacy generated excitement (and support for long-
standing staff efforts toward growth), it also increased the level of tension.

Accomplishing the culture shift required for transition to program size has taken several years of persistent effort and a cadre of leaders willing to pay the emotional cost (disapproval from some fellow members). Urgency about matters of growth is now becoming integrated into the congregation's self-understanding.

In faith traditions characterized to some significant degree by liberal theology and democratic polity[9], the authority to change size (and therefore to modify religious culture) must be "constructed" from materials at hand in the congregation's cultural "tool kit." Lay leaders and clergy proceed most wisely when they help the congregation to explore in depth its own history and religious heritage. In this process, trusted members may be able to dig out a few durable, authoritative, and widely shared congregational values to serve as the footings for cultural change. Golden Rule Christians may then be more willing to accept the challenge and pay the price. Indeed, being ready to sacrifice in times of crisis is a Golden Rule value.

Preparatory Task 3
Enriching the Congregation's Practices of Democracy and Discernment

In nearly all the churches in this study, the religious value most frequently affirmed in leader interviews and group story telling was democracy. This is partly attributable to the sample, which includes congregations that actually helped to invent the New England town meeting. However, because congregationalism has deeply influenced American religion as a whole, such adamantly democratic faith communities still have something to teach others. These churches function as "little publics," living and promoting an intense civic culture of their own. Urban sociologist Lowell Livezey[10] argues that this is one important way congregations contribute to the public good, and he commends proselytizing as an assertive way of being open and inclusive—active invitation builds the strength and diversity of the "little public." (This way of seeing evangelism may be helpful to mainline churches whose religious values have a strong civic dimension.)

In the pastoral- to program-size transition, it helps both to enrich the congregation's patterns of democratic participation and to develop (or reinforce) a complementary set of congregational practices for spiritual discernment.

Open Process

For the seven churches in the "Raising the Roof" study, democracy is a spiritual practice, and process questions carry moral weight. Change typically came about through repeated cycles of planning, decision making, and implementation. In each cycle, the congregation focused on extending their capacity in the way they believed most critical at that moment: expanding the building, adding staff, multiplying worship services, or raising capital funds. Sometimes the cycle began with work on an overall long-range plan, but sometimes proposals on a single topic (like parking) pressed the congregation toward a more comprehensive look at its life and its future. Whatever the sequence, the key to steady movement forward was an open and deliberate process, directed by respected laity with change management skills and supported by consistent clergy involvement (neither dominance nor complete delegation). Certain lay leaders functioned as "change champions" in each church—shepherding the growth project from one phase to the next and serving in a succession of growth-related leadership roles.

Moments of Truth

None of the churches made a one-time decision to "be program size." Yet each church came to at least one moment of truth—a situation or decision that became a crucial test of the congregation's willingness to change size. Pivotal events included:

- The vote to approve a building expansion or a purchase of land.
- The addition of a second major Sunday service, a decision often intertwined with choices about the participation of children. (In one case, a serious and painful conflict erupted with a motion to end the recently established second service. Charles Arn[11] has shown that this crisis is often delayed until the moment when the additional service overtakes the previous "main" service in attendance.)
- The debate over adding staff.
- Turning people away on Easter morning. (In one case, this experienced galvanized the pastor and lay leaders to take action.)

Some congregations in the study experienced more than one of these moments of truth during their sojourn in the transition zone between sizes.

Effective Advocates

The need for good process is well understood by all seven churches in the sample (even if they sometimes overlook a step or misjudge the degree of consensus). The need for effective advocacy may be a bit less obvious in these communities where "tolerance" and "diversity" are key words. Where no one expresses any passionate convictions, democratic processes have no fuel to drive them forward. Although too much heat can burn out the engine, mainline Protestants rarely suffer from an excess of fervor about seizing opportunities for growth. Each of these churches had effective advocates who persistently made the case for expanding capacity, even in the face of some anxiety and resistance. Pastors and boards in each of the study churches provided room for these advocates to raise important issues. As a degree of tension developed, leaders channeled the resulting energy into some clear structure, such as a formal planning process.

Healthy Norms for Conflict

Tension about growth stops generating useful energy when the system does not articulate and defend firm ground rules for disagreement. Two churches in the study did an exceptional job of addressing potentially volatile conflicts.

In the first case, the pastor and board referred a serious complaint about a staff member to a panel of leaders who conducted a formal inquiry—containing the dispute within firm boundaries and assuring the rest of the congregation that it was being handled responsibly. When the panel did not concur with the complaint, leaders conveyed to the aggrieved parties that the matter was closed; they did not allow the issue to fester.

In the second case, a member of the church's inner leadership circle took exception to a formal group decision and had trouble letting go of the issue even though his opinion clearly had not carried the day. In this congregation—whose dominant religious culture might be described as "liberal evangelical"—pastor and board spent time studying the standards for conflict found in Matthew 18 and communicated clearly to individual members that—after open discussion of viewpoints—the legitimate decisions of the congregation had to be respected. The pastors in both of these churches scored relatively well on both the flexibility and the effectiveness of their leadership style (as measured by the Blanchard LBA II instrument), and both tended to be proactive in the face of conflict.

In contrast, one church experienced an intense and painful growth-related conflict over the creation of a second worship service and church school program. (I have already described a bit of this fight in my discussion of Golden Rule authority.) In hindsight, the pastor and deacons believe that they overloaded the system by changing the basic order worship just before they went to the two-service schedule; this tension ultimately erupted in a bid to repeal the two-service decision. On the LBA II inventory, the pastor of this congregation rated somewhat lower on leadership flexibility. He frankly described himself to me as a person who had generally tended to avoid conflict prior to this experience. Although the system around him did not have enough compensating strengths in conflict management to prevent a painful win-lose resolution of the worship fight, the church was able to make a clear decision and move forward with its program—sometimes the most that can be achieved in particular circumstances. At the time of the interviewing, it did not appear to me that this congregation and its leaders had recovered their energy and confidence after this difficult experience. Since then, the two-service structure has taken hold and is operating well.

A congregation's ability to set healthy norms for handling disagreement is an important component of readiness for size transition. Two outstanding resources for this work are Denise Goodman's book *Congregational Fitness*[12] and Gil Rendle's *Behavioral Covenants in Congregations*.[13]

Democracy and Discernment

Author Charles Olsen and others have suggested that the great political and religious innovation of the 17th century—parliamentary governance in religious systems—may need to be enriched with classic Christian practices of spiritual discernment. Just as individual Golden Rule Christians may benefit from small group settings where they can tell and reflect upon their own faith story, whole congregations need practice in relating their local story to the great stories of faith, especially when important choices are being made. In an informal way, some of the study churches made use of a major anniversary celebration to retell the local story and to connect it with a core faith theme and a current sense of calling. One of the churches has a historical connection with the composer of the music for "Blest Be the Tie That Binds" (the tune is named for this faith community); some leaders see that particular hymn as emblematic of the congregation's character. But with more explicit and consistent practices of spiritual discernment, these and other churches might add another dimension to their decision making and gain greater confidence about articulating their special vocation.

PREPARATORY TASK 4
ASSESSING THE CONGREGATION'S PROGRESS ON KEY DIMENSIONS OF SYSTEM CHANGE

Generally speaking, pastors and lay leaders underestimate the scope and extent of change that is required before a congregation hits its stride with a program way of operating. Without an accurate inventory of the degree and kind of change involved, leaders cannot solicit informed consent from the congregation. Even more fundamentally, leaders cannot properly assess their own commitment and capacity to see this transition through.

In appendix A, I have listed nine dimensions of organizational change required in order to complete the transition from a pastoral to a program way of being church. The full inventory is will soon be available as part of an Alban resource for congregations navigating the pastoral- to program-size transition. Gary McIntosh provides another way to measure size-related organizational change in his book *One Size Doesn't Fit All*.[14]

CONCLUSION

Although a pastoral- to program-size change is an especially difficult transition, healthy churches in growing communities can indeed step up to this challenge. The four preparatory tasks described here can lay the groundwork for effective congregational discernment and action.

APPENDIX A

FACTORS IN THE SYSTEM CHANGE INDEX

Factor 1: **Congregational self-definition.** The story leaders tell about the congregation's size and character. Language and images used. Functioning theology about size and growth.

Factor 2: **Pastor's role.** Emphasis on pastor's role as leader, equipper, and organizer. Ability and willingness to delegate. Understanding and acceptance of this role by lay leaders and members.

Factor 3: **Size of paid staff.** A pastoral-size church may expect to operate well with a full-time pastor and a part-time musician as program staff. Congregations in the pastoral- to program-size transition need additional paid staff (programmatic, secretarial, accounting, and custodial) in order to create capacity for growth.

Factor 4: **Optimum unfilled capacity at our main Sabbath services/ programs.** Maximum opportunity for growth when 30 to 40 percent of the comfortable seating capacity is still unfilled at every major Sabbath service. Parking, education, and fellowship areas should also have obvious unfilled capacity every week. These factors affect participation level of current members as well as permeability to newcomers.

Factor 5: **Degree of movement toward multicell reality.** In a growing pastoral-size church, the same small network of leaders often becomes stressed as it tries keep everything going. They still provide the emotional glue that holds the church together as a single circle of fellowship. In a multicelled congregation, the informal network is replaced by fully functioning boards and committees that draw new leaders from all parts of the congregation. Members accept the fact that there are distinct subcommunities within the church—often assembled around multiple major Sabbath worship services.

Factor 6: **Delegation of planning and change management tasks to special groups with appropriate gifts.** Timely progression from planning studies to decision to implementation, including fund development. Adequate number of self-motivated lay leaders ("change champions") guiding the political and organizational processes from phase to phase and integrating the work into a coherent effort. Willingness to learn from outside sources.

Factor 7: **Growing aspirations to quality.** Especially in the worship experience (preaching, music, children's participation, cohesion of elements, climate of hospitality), nursery and education for children, education/spiritual development of adults, and major community programming (such as singles group, weekday nursery school).

Factor 8: **Infrastructure for member care and involvement.** Many gifted teams working on the tasks of new member incorporation, pastoral care, small groups, larger fellowship occasions, and ongoing "member ministry development" (gift-identification, volunteer management, support for ministry in daily life). Reliable member database constantly updated, accessible to all leaders as needed.

Factor 9: **Conflict prevention and management.** Communication among different groups and functions. Settings where "pinches" are identified early and addressed through shared problem solving. Board and clergy competence in managing conflicts that arise. High commitment to due process. Attention to restoring energy and trust after a difficult fight.

Appendix B
Factors in the Stevenson
"Margin-in-Life" Scale[15]

Factor 1: Health   Contains the body (physical) items as well as mental and general health items.

Factor 2: Self   Includes items about responsibility, work life, life goals, ability to concentrate, self-confidence, adaptability to change, decision making, and temper-control.

Factor 3: Family   Contains items concerned with the family as a whole, with children and spouses specifically, and with other relatives.

Factor 4: Religiosity/ Spirituality   Contains religiosity items, which deal with the dimensions of an organized religion, such as church membership, prayer, Bible reading, people met at church and through church-related activities. Includes spirituality items: philosophy of life, honesty, conscience, and a personal value system.

Factor 5: Community   Contains items about the larger environment; keeping abreast of world and local news, items about neighbors and civic activities.

Appendix C
"Raising the Roof" Interview Questions

1. **Person Interviewed**
   a. Name
   b. Phone number
   c. How long attending
   d. Current church position(s)
   e. Past church positions
   f. Approximate age
   g. (Added informally professional background)

2. **Size History of Congregation**
I would like to understand the history of this church's thinking about growth and size change.
   a. Any initial comments?
   b. How long ago did this church start grappling with these issues? How?
   c. Is there a particular moment or event that really put questions of growth or size on the table? How?
   d. Have there ever been "camps" of opinion about whether to grow or how to grow? What were they?
   e. On a scale of 1 to 10 (one is low), how controversial has this subject been in the past five years?

3. **Leadership**
I assume that growth and size change requires leadership from many different places.
   a. Initial comments on who has been leading the church to grow or change size? How how this been done?
   b. Comments on the role of senior pastor?
   c. Moderator?
   d. Primary governing board?
   e. Committees and task forces?
   f. Other individuals?

4. Individual Role

I'd like to understand where you fit into this story.

    a. Initial comments?

    b. When did you first become conscious of this church's choices about growth and size? How?

    c. What have you done about those issues?

5. Conflict

    a. On a scale of 1 to 10 (1 is low), how much conflict or disagreement has there been about these issues?

    b. When did people fight or disagree?

    c. How was this handled?

6. Authority

Growth involves change. Change means giving up some treasured ways of doing things. Some leaders ask: "What right do I have to ask others in this church to change?"

    a. Any thoughts?

    b. Have others ever questioned your position or wisdom on this issue?

    c. To what extent do you feel you have the right or responsibility to put growth or size change on the church's agenda?

    d. I'd like to understand the foundation on which you stand. Please rate each statement 1 to 10 (1 means low agreement with the statement).

        1. As I see it, seeking to grow is a good business strategy for the church.

        2. As I see it, seeking to grow is a biblical mandate.

        3. As I see it, seeking to grow is not an issue at all—we're just trying to manage the problems that are right in front of us.

        4. As I see it, people need spiritual help in their lives. We're supposed to find the people who need that help and offer it.

        5. As I see it, my life was changed when somebody helped me find faith. I'm supposed to do that for others.

        6. As I see it, the judicatory has growth as a goal, and we should cooperate with that work.

        7. As I see it, being a called or elected leader means taking some heat around hard issues, including growth.

        8. As I see it, leaders should only do what the congregation wants or seems comfortable with.

9. (For lay leaders) As I see it, our minister believes we should grow and I think we should cooperate with that effort.

7. Other
What else should I have asked? What other comments would you like to make?

NOTES

1. Linda J. Clark, Joanne Swenson, and Mark Stamm, *How We Seek God Together: Exploring Worship Style* (Bethesda, Md.: The Alban Institute, 2001), chapter 2.

2. Carl Dudley, William McKinney, and Jackson Carroll, *Handbook for Congregational Studies* (Nashville: Abingdon Press, 1986), pp. 29-30.

3. Anne Swidler, "Culture in Action: Symbols and Strategies," in *American Sociological Review* (April 1986).

4. Nancy T. Ammerman, "Spiritual Journeys in the American Mainstream," in *Congregations* (January/February 1997), pp. 11-15.

5. The study included a group exploration of the congregation's history, plus individual interviews with the (full-time) pastors and two lay leaders in each church. The questions I asked in the individual interviews are found in appendix C.

6. Joanne Sabol Stevenson, "Construction of a Scale to Measure Load, Power and Margin in Life," *Nursing Research* 31, no. 4 (July/August 1982).

7. Celia Allison Hahn, *Growing in Authority, Relinquishing Control* (Bethesda, Md.: The Alban Institute, 1994), p. 28.

8. *Leader Behavior Analysis II* (Escondido, Calif.: The Ken Blanchard Companies, 1999).

9. "Liberal" and "democratic" are relative terms. But even Protestant denominations with a hierarchical structure–Episcopal, Presbyterian, United Methodist, for example–still rely on elected governing boards and (on some issues) congregational meetings to authorize important changes.

10. This concept of the congregation as a "little public" comes from the work of the Religion in Urban America Program of the University of Illinois at Chicago, which since 1992 has studied the experiences of some 75 congregations in the metropolitan area. Lowell W. Livezey directs the program. The Alban Institute will publish learnings from this work in late 2001.

11. Charles Arn, "Multiple Worship Services and Church Growth," in *Journal of the American Institute of Church Growth* 7 (1996), p. 96.

12. Denise W. Goodman, *Congregational Fitness: Healthy Practices for Layfolk* (Bethesda, Md.: The Alban Institute, 2000).

13. Gilbert R. Rendle, *Behavioral Covenants in Congregations: A Handbook for Honoring Differences* (Bethesda, Md.: The Alban Institute, 1999).

14. Gary L. McIntosh, *One Size Doesn't Fit All* (Grand Rapids, Mich.: Baker Books, 1999), pp. 46-48.

15. Stevenson, "Construction of a Scale," p. 22.

Excerpted from Raising the Roof: The Pastoral-to-Program Size Transition *(Bethesda, Md.: The Alban Institute, 2001).*

CHAPTER 9

One Size Doesn't Fit All

Reflections on Becoming a Corporate-Size Church

Joel S. McCoy

Many churches and their leaders find the myriad of books and articles related to church growth both daunting and confusing. After reading almost any of these books, church leaders might end up feeling guilty that their church is not growing in size. The stories offered in these books seem to fit other situations or leaders, and leave readers confused about what size their church can and should become.

That said, I would recommend Gary L. McIntosh's *One Size Doesn't Fit All: Bringing Out the Best in Any Size Church* (Baker, 1999). This book will assist any size church and its leaders to clearly identify their congregation's type and will explain how the congregation can become the best it can be.

McIntosh delineates three different types of churches, based on worship attendance. If a church averages between 15 and 200 worshippers on Sunday morning, McIntosh identifies it as a "small church." A church that averages between 201 and 400 worshippers is a "medium church." If a church averages 401 worshippers or more, McIntosh identifies that as a "large church."

Arlin Rothauge's theory of congregational sizes, the theory perhaps most familiar to leaders of mainline Protestant congregations, differs from McIntosh's. Rothauge identifies four sizes. Churches with up to 50 active worshippers are "family" or "patriarchal/matriarchal" churches, and those with between 50 and 150 active worshippers are "pastoral" churches. If average worship attendance falls between 150 and 350, he calls the church a "program church." He labels a congregation with over 350 active worshippers a "corporate church."

McIntosh presents a chart of his categories, a useful tool called "Typology of Church Size." Included in this chart is his outline of ten factors or

phases he believes can be identified in any size church: relational orientation, structural type, leadership mechanism, pastoral role, decision-making
processes, staff impact, change process, growth patterns, growth obstacles,
and growth strategies. McIntosh elaborates on these factors in separate
chapters, each with a question as its title to help the reader understand the
role of the factor.

McIntosh contends that these ten factors can be used to identify the
unique needs of different size churches. He believes that "for church leaders to be effective they must understand that churches have different needs
depending on size.... Specific strategies for different size churches are necessary. Church leaders build on this fact."[1]

McIntosh's explanation of these factors will make you feel like he has
been in your church. He does a brilliant job of drawing you into the material
by presenting it through the eyes of a young pastor in a small church. This
pastor discovers a mentor in an older pastor, who walks him through
McIntosh's information. Most church leaders will be able to relate to the
young pastor's efforts to understand his size church and will be encouraged
by his struggles to take an honest look at size.

McIntosh says 80 percent of churches are small; 10 percent are medium; and 10 percent are large. Therefore, most readers of his book will
relate best to the factors of the small church. However, the church I serve
is on the precipice between the medium- and large-size church. Working
through the transition to the large size has proved to be a great challenge.
But McIntosh's list of key factors has offered significant insight and has
become a valuable analytical tool for all our congregation's leaders as we
have sought to break through (to use Rothauge's categories) the program-
size barrier to become a corporate-size church.

In my experience, some of the factors McIntosh has identified are
more crucial than others in the transition process. Six factors presented the
greatest challenges, and working through them required much time, prayer,
and patience. We have not conquered these issues but continue to work
through this transition. What follows are my impressions and insights, formed
both from McIntosh's work and from understandings I have gleaned while
working through this transition process.

THE STRETCHED CELL

This factor involves the stress people experience in the way they relate to each other. McIntosh says single-cell systems will feel stretched when they try to grow and necessarily become multicell systems. In our congregation, stress points were manifested in three arenas. First, people had difficulty maintaining trusting and loving relationships. Their relational anxieties were exhibited in a resounding ambivalence toward change, which in turn was demonstrated in their willingness to accept their relational weakness as well as their reluctance to grow into a larger, multicell congregation. The irony of this condition is that members perceived themselves to be part of a friendly and caring church.

Many people operate in a constant state of unhappiness with someone or some church program. In our congregation, this unhappiness easily became the context for the way many people related—a second manifestation of this stretched-cell orientation. Some individuals became the lieutenants of unhappiness and saw their role as maintaining a tension and anxiety level characteristic of the stretched cell. Ironically, they often perceived themselves as helping the church follow the will of God and preserve its history.

Third, the history of our church reflects tensions and anxiety. My review of the church board minutes of the past twenty-five years evidenced that policy-type decisions were often made in reaction to high anxiety in the life of the church. These high-anxiety issues tended to be overblown rather than prayerfully and rationally approached. Our history, then, fits the stretched-cell experience McIntosh describes.

McIntosh compares the tension within the stretched-cell congregation with the tension on a rubber band, which must remain under pressure in order for the rubber band to remain stretched. The pressure needed to maintain this size church is the very thing that prevents it from making the transition to the large church structure. I have both observed and felt that pressure in our church. For example, the sheer number of programs required to keep the medium-size church functioning became one of our greatest obstacle in making the transition to the large church with a multicell structure. A specific issue in our setting was that some people viewed their favorite program as the one that *must* be preserved, and they responded to the perceived threat to the program with great defensiveness.

In addition, most of the church programs were still served by a small percentage of the congregation's members. They supported new opportunities for ministry involving new people as long as the new leaders did not serve on the more prestigious and powerful committees. New people were allowed to serve in only a limited number of programs that afforded them low levels of control. Leadership of power committees still belonged to certain key members who knew how the church was "supposed" to operate. Some of these key members even approached me to explain that these committees should be reserved for those who are more knowledgeable about the church.

Overall, members had a difficult time either letting programs die or involving new people. Many well-established programs became nostalgic rehearsals of their glory days. Members spent much time and energy yearning for the return of these programs and ministries. Many people had a hard time getting beyond this nostalgia.

THE ROLE OF THE PASTOR

The three distinct ways church people view their pastor are key size indicators, according to McIntosh. He says the small church needs a "lover," the medium church needs an "administrator," and the large church needs a "leader." For each size church, people have definite expectations concerning the role of their pastor.

Our church is made up of members with backgrounds from all three church sizes, and it is my observation that members expect their pastor to be just like the pastor of the church size they have experienced in the past. Such mixed expectations would result in role confusion for any pastor attempting to lead a transition into becoming a large church. I have dealt with the uncertainty brought about by the expectations of these members and have often found myself confused about which pastoral roles I should fulfill. An understanding of our congregation's size and the pastoral role needed has been critical to my dealing with these expectations.

This insight can prevent pastors who are attempting to make the transition into the large-size church from being overcome by discouragement and fear. Most pastors want to be the Messiah who does everything, and that dream seems to prevent them from adjusting their pastoral role according to their congregation's size. Pastors discover that learning to limit themselves to the leadership style needed by their particular congregation offers a great challenge. Further, McIntosh perceptively observes that most pastors begin serving in small churches and have a difficult time adjusting their leadership style as they move or their congregation grows into medium and large sizes.

My experience has been consistent with what McIntosh describes. Some lay leaders wanted me to adapt my role to meet the size they wanted our church to become—not necessarily a large church! It was difficult for me to deal with these pressures while trying to help us make the transition through the many difficulties we experienced. I now understand McIntosh to say, however, that the pastors do not cease serving as lover or administrator when the leadership role requirements change with the church's size. Rather, the needs of the church and its members, shaped by their particular size, frame the *primary* role the pastor should exercise. Pastors must continue to use the gifts and skills they have developed in smaller congregations, but the focus changes to address the church's changing needs. Consequently, the greatest challenge for the pastor becomes developing the appropriate *new* pastoral skills to lead the church through the transition to the next size. Meeting this challenge requires a willingness to learn and change ways of thinking and feeling. My counsel is that conviction and courage will be required, if you believe God is leading you and your church through a size transition.

CHANGE AND THE ISSUE OF TRUST

Congregations that are willing to make the medium- to large-church transition will face great resistance to change. This resistance is inevitable in the church that tries to change the power structures of the church. As churches move into the large-church category, rather than exercising power and bringing about change through a bureaucracy of key committees, deacon boards, or other groups, change must begin to occur through the initiation of the senior pastor, who is joined by gifted staff members and lay leaders. A team approach involving the senior pastor, gifted staff members, and equipped lay leaders needs to be created. This approach streamlines the church and shakes up the power structures already in place.

Adapting the committee structure in particular is essential to making a successful transition. This adapting does not mean committees cease to serve, but that they adjust their ways of operating. Leaders must be motivated by a heart to serve people, rather than the exercise of power. I have observed two factors that challenge the committee-run church and that a congregation must face before this change can take place.

First, a congregation must clarify whether members can trust God to lead them through the change process. They need to ask, What does God want this church to be? When a church clearly answers this question, McIntosh believes purpose and vision statements then need to be developed. These statements reveal how the congregation views itself and its role in the community.

Once confidence in God's leadership for the church is established, the second factor involves the pastor and staff. A trust relationship between the pastor, other staff, and members must be developed before a change in structure can happen. Due to difficult staff relationships in our congregation's past, many of our members were suspicious of any changes suggested by their pastor or staff, and consequently, some people became very critical of both staff and changes. The changes threatened the keepers of the church's history and the people in existing positions of power. As it became clear that some people might have to give up positions of control, fear clouded the power brokers' reactions, judgments, and spiritual discernment. I believe this factor is especially an issue in older, more established churches like the one I serve. Evaluating and changing the familiar decision-making processes meant challenging and educating the congregation. (This happened as I used Alice Mann's *The In-Between Church* to teach staff and members about size transitions, and invited Alice to consult with us on these transition issues.)

THE CHURCH STAFF

McIntosh poses a question important to the size transition between the medium and large church: "Is the church staffed to decline, remain on a plateau, or grow?"[2] How a congregation answers this question is crucial, because the growth of the church depends on adding staff, and adding staff is a daunting challenge. Real financial strain is the major issue most churches face when they are deciding whether to add staff. McIntosh contends that when a church waits until it can afford another staff member, the growth opportunities have by then become limited. Hesitation in taking a faith step and providing financially for a new staff member can keep a church stuck on a plateau between medium and large sizes and prevent it from reaching to become a large church.

There is a delicate line between having the faith to grow and facing the reality of the issues, and I can affirm the difficulty of balancing financial issues and faith steps. My church dealt with these issues a few years ago when we voted to hire a fourth full-time staff member. Financial issues were the limiting factor as we contemplated filling that position, and I agree with McIntosh that finances can become the primary reason for not hiring new staff. In my experience, the decision to add staff is a real and continuing struggle that can only be solved when congregations have the courage earnestly to seek and trust the provision of God.

Another daunting aspect of the staffing issue is how the new staff members will work with the existing staff members and the members of the church. Most pastors have probably discovered that finding staff members whose gifts, personality, and work ethic complement the staff team is one of the most difficult areas of the pastorate. As the prospective staff member is considered, the gracious calling of God must be clear to the pastor and church, so they can work together to build the kingdom of God. In the end, however, the pastor and church must successfully work together to add staff before the transition to the next size can be completed.

McIntosh comments on the struggle to add staff:

> For a church to make the transition from the medium church to a large church, it will normally take a staff of four to five pastors plus additional support staff. Be aware, though, that moving from a small staff of three pastors to a multiple staff of four pastors is a difficult transition. In fact, this is one of the barriers to moving past four hundred worshippers.[3]

McIntosh, Alice Mann, and Alban senior consultant Roy Oswald all agree that as a rule of thumb, if a congregation wants to staff for growth, it needs one full-time program person on the staff for every one hundred active members. (Mann believes, it should be noted, that the rule of thumb refers to all professional staff in a congregation, not just to ordained clergy. It is not clear how McIntosh views this matter.)

I suggest caution when beginning the process of adding new staff members. A clear direction can be defined by asking questions such as, How many staff are needed? And what type of staff position is required at this point in our history? Both the perceived and the real needs of the church must be clarified for effective staffing to take place.

PROGRAM-TO-PROCLAMATION MODEL

Another challenge for the church making a size transition is growing from a program-oriented model of growth to a proclamation-oriented model. In my view, the focus on programs becomes a significant obstacle when making the transition to the next size level. Growth occurs in the program model by adding programs. This orientation can become a hindrance when the congregation develops programs to reach people rather than assisting people to reach others. The proclamation model expands the program focus and actively involves the members, who begin to reach others through community-based ministry and outreach as well as through person-to-person influence.

In medium-size program churches, people tend to expect the pastor and staff to start new ministry programs. As the church approaches the transition to becoming a large church, the dependence on staff-driven programs must change. Members may become reluctant to accept the large-church proclamation model, which the staff must adopt when trying to implement the size transition, and then staff-member relationships can become strained. Maintaining the program model becomes harder, however, as awareness grows that the church should make the transition to the large church. During this period of tension, many staff members burn out under the stress of this tug-of-war. The church that approaches the upper limits of the medium-size church has already begun to experience these large-church stress points.

My church has experienced this stress. The people have been reluctant to become instruments of proclamation. Changing from a come-and-see-us mentality to a go-and-tell approach has proven challenging. Members' reasons for reluctance include too much knowledge of the community, fear of trying, and an unwillingness to stretch beyond their comfort level.

LONG-RANGE PLANNING

One of the crucial growth strategies McIntosh presents is writing a long-range plan. In my experience, there are some key challenges to completing a long-range plan. The first challenge is to help members of medium-size churches learn to think like large-church members. People find it difficult to break out of their established stereotypes about church, which keep them from breaking through to think like members of a large church. During a recent conversation, the most frequent comment about our church's future had to do with the need for survival. This thinking was alarming to the staff and me. The potential for reaching new people and changing structures had not yet affected their thinking to the extent needed if we were to become a large church.

The second challenge is to learn to focus on strengths rather than congregational weaknesses and historical problems. Church people have long memories and react if they sense an unpleasant experience might recur. An unwillingness to address these old issues becomes a limiting factor when attempting to think creatively and begin the long-range planning required to reach the next size. I believe it is essential to work through the grief and hurt of past experiences if effective and efficient long-range planning is to take place. This grief work can take anywhere from a few hours of dialogue to several sessions, depending on how deeply the grief and hurt are imbedded.

Our church has held such conversation for healing. Clear rules were set out at the beginning of the process. We agreed to spend more time listening than reacting or defending. A trusted consultant was brought in to lead this dialogue with the entire congregation. Before the consultant arrived, an oversight group participated in dialogue. Past hurts were openly shared, and people began to listen to each other. The conversation touched and united hearts as we dealt with the grief of our church's past.

After such issues are discussed—in our case, following our guided dialogue—a calendar mapping a plan for dreaming about the future and developing a long-range strategy can be put in place. Then the congregation can work within that framework to build a long-range plan around its strengths and potential that is consistent with its mission and personality. Members can begin asking, What do we do best? What the church does best provides opportunity for celebration and excitement in both the planning and implementation of the long-range plan and a successful transition to the next size.

MY RECOMMENDATIONS

I suggest congregational leaders develop a plan to help staff and members learn about and discuss the commitment required to make the transition to a large church. Books such as *One Size Doesn't Fit All* by McIntosh and

The In-Between Church by Mann are excellent resources for the education process. Congregational leaders must carefully study the issues of size transition, especially if the congregation is moving from being a medium-size to a large church. One-on-one conversations and small group dialogues among leaders and other members will also be helpful. In particular, the transition from a program orientation to a proclamation orientation must be openly and honestly discussed. The type of changes required must be identified, and a time line for the changes should be laid out.

A healthy transition can be achieved if both staff and members are patient and cooperative. The challenges are numerous, and the way can be slippery. Ingrained patterns are difficult to change. However, the grace of God will be sufficient when you and your church place your confidence in God to lead you through these issues of transition.

NOTES

1. Gary L. McIntosh, *One Size Doesn't Fit All: Bringing Out the Best in Any Size Church* (Grand Rapids, Mich.: Baker Books, 1999), p.19.
2. Ibid., p. 88.
3. Ibid., p. 94.

CHAPTER 10

Marks of Growing Churches

The Confederate Approach to Church Growth

G. W. Garvin

Is it true that only conservative churches are growing? As a pastor who loves the mainline tradition with its roots in the compelling biblical images of reconciliation, inclusiveness, and human concern, I am haunted by this question. Equally frightening is the unspoken assumption that mainline churches are relics of the past that are inevitably declining, uninspiring in a cynical era, and doomed to die. Like many ministers, I am concerned about the future of the local church, which I love, where I work, and which provides a vision worth committing my life to. It was this compelling concern that led me on a quest to discover anything and everything that I could about the prospects for the mainline local church.

Reading the literature on church growth was at first an exercise in despair. I soon found the seminary bookshelves to be loaded with writings that confirmed the conservative bias. Only conservative churches are growing, and only a conservative approach will work. Despite my disappointment, I was determined to read all the literature, whether it appealed to my instincts or not. Eventually it became clear that much of the writing was rooted in the pioneering efforts of Donald McGavran, former Dean of the School of World Mission, Fuller Theological Seminary. An ingenious pragmatist, McGavran illustrated how church growth had taken place in world missions. Other early work on church growth focused on whole denominations and churches compared to each other on a national and international scale. But I wanted to learn about the local church and congregation. In the case of my own congregation, is it possible to turn around thirty years of statistical decline and achieve numerical growth?

Hope for Mainline Churches

I eventually found two pearls of great value not under the sections on church growth, but under the rubric of renewal. *What's Ahead for Old First Church* by Ezra Earl Jones and Robert L. Wilson and *New Hope for Congregations* by Loren Mead blended careful analysis with illustrations of renewal and vitality. Both books told stories. They were based not in philosophical arguments, but in the grassroots world of congregations facing contemporary issues and problems. They are case studies of real churches and demonstrate that, to a remarkable degree, every congregation must do its own soul searching and find its own way to growth.

These books told me that mainline churches are growing. They suggested that, although each church must work out its own methods and programs, certain general principles are present in all growing congregations. And these principles are critical to growth!

I set out to explore whether these principles were true in my own denomination and what was actually happening statistically to congregations. I analyzed the statistical data of large West Coast Presbyterian churches and determined which were growing, which were static, and which were declining.

Much to my surprise, many stereotypes proved to be myths. Many large conservative churches with national reputations for growth were actually in decline, or at best stable. At the same time, many large mainline churches, located in the complex environments of urban areas, were growing. After I had compiled the data on all the churches, I made a second surprising discovery. The proportion of churches marked by growth or decline proved to be approximately equal. In other words, for every conservative church that was growing, there was a mainline congregation that was also growing. The results for declining churches were similar. For every mainline church that was in decline, there was a conservative one to match it. Perhaps it is time for someone to write a book titled *Why Mainline Churches Are Growing!*

What could the pastors of these large growing mainline churches tell me about church growth? It was the quest for the answer to this question that led me to a series of interviews that provided helpful insight into the dynamics of growth. These interviews were the culmination of my probe into growth concerns that included a large reading list of books and articles, as well as a hard-nosed statistical analysis of congregations. After digesting this material, I discovered there are indeed principles that can be used as benchmarks for congregations in search of growth and revitalization.

THE CONFEDERATE APPROACH

Perhaps it is the theology of conservative churches that compels them to develop "the" solution to most of the mysteries of life. Although the conservative tradition might be marked by its tendency to believe that it has "the way," "the answer," or "the solution" for everything from child grooming to church growth, in fact, there is another way! This approach might be called the "confederate approach to church growth." The confederate approach is rooted in the preference of the mainline tradition to acknowledge and even relish the diversity of viewpoint in the life of the congregation.

What are the principles and hallmarks of mainline congregations that are growing? Churches that grow articulate a distinct and winsome identity. They develop a unifying vision. Developing this vision is the primary task for the leaders of these growing congregations. The task falls primarily on the shoulders of the minister who is head of staff and secondarily on the leadership core of the congregation. This leadership core is composed of the rest of the professional staff and key lay leaders.

A vision is not the same thing as a program. As one pastor said, "There is a difference between selling and articulating a vision. A vision must have roots in the congregation. Vision makes the congregation's mouth water." The leaders regard this task as a joy, not a burden. Generally, growing churches are inclined to draw a vision from the congregation rather than push a program on a congregation.

The central vision for many of these churches is focused on the larger world. One of these pastors described his congregation by saying, "Our church has a global preoccupation." Another pastor described their task as "seeing the church as part of the whole." In a remarkable fashion these congregations were able to blend the unique quality of their congregation with a deep commitment to a larger world purpose. This blending of the local uniqueness with a high sense of Christian global purpose creates a winsome magnetic quality in their congregations. In general, these large growing congregations blend a sense of unique local identity with a global perspective that is both sensitive to and aligned with the denominational concern for international perspectives.

A second principle that emerged is developing skill and openness in managing conflict. The two phrases I heard most often in the interviews with pastors were "working for consensus" and "not making unilateral decisions." The pastor of a church where controversial issues play an important role in the life of the congregation and provide a focus for their congregational life says, "We don't have many showdowns."

Most pastors interviewed were very process sensitive. As one pastor described his church, "It's like a turtle. Once in a while it sticks its neck out on an issue, and then when it gets bruised, it backs off for a while." These congregations have learned to enjoy their diversity, rather than deny it. They were marked by the ability to work their way through differences, with an ability to come to creative compromises or exchanges that made most participants feel that they had not been painted into a corner or backed up against a wall. Generally speaking, most members were able to feel that they had not participated in win-lose or lose-lose situations.

The relationship between pastor and laity is critical to successful conflict management. At times, the heart of the solution is in the attitude of the pastor toward the leader. One pastor said, "We believe strong leadership is in concert with strong laity." The impression is given that these congregations are not reluctant to tackle controversial issues. Yet they are sensitive to the need for dialogue and integrity through conflicting ideas. Diversity and conflict are united in such a way that they become strengths.

The third principle that marks growing churches is quality program development. Quality, however, was the only common ingredient. Growing churches have many different programs that are as diverse as the communities they serve. One pastor said, "Growth is the product of not one, but a constellation of strategies." I discovered that these churches had developed no less than twenty-two strategies. Diversity means providing many points of entry and addressing the diverse needs of the community. Program development is not treated passively. It is an active concern. A critical question is, How many points of entry does this program provide?

Christian education is undergoing a change in many congregations. A striking number of congregations do not provide traditional patterns of children's and young people's programs. These churches have moved past the post-World War II American religion boom, when Christian education programs were developed as easily as falling off a log. These churches develop a sense of their own identity and then develop appropriate education programs that blend with the larger purpose. Having a successful (read between the lines "big") program is never the goal or purpose. One sure-fire way to determine if a church is in decline is to ask the leaders, What is your goal or purpose? If the answer is "growth" or "numbers," you probably have a church in decline. Aggressive outreach is always the "strategy" and never the "goal" of a growing church!

With few exceptions these growing churches have developed multiple offerings in music and choirs as the major thrust of program development for strategic growth. No group offers more points of entry and quicker assimilation than a choir program. In addition, music is a very winsome feature in church promotion. The music programs of growing churches are always described as "excellent" or "superb." When asked the question, "How do most people come to your church?" one pastor replied; "Most were attracted through the choirs." Growing churches today have replaced a historic emphasis on children's education with an emphasis on the arts. In growing churches there was no reference whatsoever to the infamous battles between choirs and ministers. Instead, frequent reference to good relations between choir programs and leadership marks nearly all these congregations.

Assimilation groups provide the fourth key factor in growing churches. Assimilation groups are most important for growth. Growing churches are marked by an intangible quality; they are "people places." The pastors blend the qualities of being process oriented and people oriented. In the confederate approach people are attracted by a sense of community. It is what one pastor called "gossip evangelism"–the natural instinct of people to share good news. Growing churches emphasize natural enthusiasm and commitment of members as opposed to advertising budgets to bring people into the life of the church. These churches enjoy being aggressive about sharing their church.

In summary, mainline churches, including large congregations in urban areas, are experiencing renewal and growth by a confederate approach. In this confederate approach the pastor and leaders join to articulate a distinctive and winsome identity (a unifying vision), provide an umbrella for diversity (conflict is resolved and consensus is achieved), develop quality programs (especially music) with many points of entry and assimilation; and encourage aggressive outreach among members as well as programs.

My personal journey of exploring the real stories and struggles of congregations in search of renewal and growth has led me to good news, and like all good news, it begs to be told. It is not true that only conservative churches are growing. It is not true that churches grow only in homogeneous communities and environments. It is true that mainline congregations with remarkable diversity, inspiring convictions, and deep seated social and human concerns are alive, well, and growing.

From Action Information, *11, no. 5 (August/September 1985): pp. 1-3.*

CHAPTER 11

Dreaming of Cathedrals, Building Skyscrapers

Discovering What It Means to Be Church

Elizabeth I. Steele

Why is it that in a time when interest in religion and spirituality is growing, participation in congregations is decline? It is not just participation in mainline congregations that is down, for despite notable exceptions, overall participation in congregational life continues to decline. Every year fewer people are attending and involved with churches.

This end-of-the-year review at First Church is typical:

Several members of the planning committee and the pastor were meeting. Sighing, Pastor J. said, "Well, another year gone by. Once again we haven't done badly, though we have not done very well either. I looked over our membership numbers. We gained almost as many as we lost, so we're holding fairly steady in numbers. Given what's happening to a lot of congregations, that's doing pretty well. What disturbs me is how we've lost people. A number of losses are due to the deaths of older members, and that's to be expected; a few more are from people moving out of the area, and we can't do anything about that either. But too many are people who just drifted away."

John, the chairperson, replied, "I know what you mean, Pastor. Betty contacted many of those whose names we're removing from the roll. They didn't express any particular upset, but they just aren't interested anymore. They make lots of different comments about spending time with their families or relaxing from work, but the bottom line seems to be that coming to church just isn't worth the effort. They don't seem to feel there's anything worth coming for."

"Our finances reflect a similar attitude. I guess I should be grate-
ful the numbers are not declining, but even when you add in the
special mission gifts, our giving is just so-so. There's nothing really
irritating people so they withhold their gifts, but there's nothing
getting them so excited they're reaching for their pocketbooks
either," commented the treasurer, Joan.

"You know, Pastor, your comment in last Sunday's sermon about
being neither hot nor cold really sums up this congregation. We're
just drifting along, not upsetting anyone but not exciting them either. It's kind of disappointing when you think about the past."

For many people, participating in a congregation is not attractive. Indeed, it is often viewed negatively. Kathleen Norris describes this response
in her book *Cloister Walk*.

One woman wrote to me to say that she felt a great longing for
ritual and community; she said she wanted to mark the year with
more than watching the trees change. She had joined some political organizations and a women's service club but found that it was
not enough. She was afraid to even think of joining a church–the
Bible makes her angry, more often than not–but she thought she
might have to.[1]

"Afraid" and "might have to" are words burdened with a sense of
inevitable discouragement. Joining a congregation is not viewed as a hope-
ful choice, one filled with possibilities and opportunities for growth, but as
something one does because there are no better options available. It is a
choice to be made in desperation, with minimal expectations for the outcome. This sense of disappointment has become so common that many
people expect it. It is frustrating for members, and the frustration increases
when intensive planning efforts fail to make a difference.

John continued, "I thought things would be different after the planning we did last year. The visitation you organized gave every
member a chance to say what we need, and we built our efforts
around their comments. People said we needed more Bible studies, so we organized them, but every class petered out after just a
few weeks."

"The same thing happened with worship," said Pastor J. "People said they wanted more meaningful worship, but no one could make particular suggestions, and everything we tried brought lots of complaints and little enthusiasm."

Joan laughed sadly, "Remember the cantata fiasco? People said we needed a strong music program, so the choir worked for weeks on that service. Then people complained about not having a sermon, and both giving and attendance went down.

"Well, Pastor, where did we go wrong? Why didn't even our big planning effort change things? Why are things so bland?"

WHY HOPEFUL PLANNING CAN FAIL

There is an old maxim about being careful how you phrase your questions, because how you ask defines the answers. One of the reasons people are drifting away from congregations is that we have been asking the wrong questions. We have been asking congregations to define their lives by setting goals and objectives and looking at people's needs, while overlooking people's dreams. Needs are not dreams. Anyone who has been on a diet understands that. Munching celery sticks because you need to lose weight does not satisfy dreams of pepperoni pizza and hot fudge sundaes.

The same is true of congregations. Congregations that structure their lives around people's needs, without considering their dreams of what congregational life could be, are not satisfying. It does not matter how good the planning process is. If people's dreams are not taken into consideration and reflected in the congregation's goals, members will be dissatisfied. Eventually many will drift away.

Even if a congregation's goals reflect the dreams of its members, its day-to-day life and decision making must be in sync with those dreams and goals, or there will still be a gap that can cause disappointment. First Church learned that when they redid their planning process.

Betty commented, "Going back and asking people what they wanted from the congregation, what they dream of, instead of what they need, sure gave us different answers and different directions for our planning."

"Yeah," said John, "but things haven't really changed much. We may know what people want, but it's still not happening."

"I know, and I'm trying to understand why," said Joan.

"That's easy," said Pastor J., "we haven't changed our habits yet."

"What do you mean?"

"People say they want to be nurtured in their faith, to understand how to pray and encounter God in their own lives. Part of that nurturing includes being visited when things aren't going well, but no one wants to do the visiting. If I'm doing it all, when do I have time to prepare and teach the class on prayer people are asking for?"

"For that matter," commented Joan, "if we ask you to do all the prayers at meetings, when do we practice the kind of praying we say we want to do?"

"Precisely."

"Pastor, remember when you said that what we'd been doing in the past was the equivalent of dreaming of a cathedral but drawing up plans for a skyscraper?" said John. "Now we have plans for a cathedral, but out of habit we are building a skyscraper anyway, just because . . ."

Everyone laughed as they said in unison, "That's the way we've always done it."

Dreams, goals, and day-to-day decision making all have to work together for a congregation to go anywhere. Imagine, for a moment, children playing with a rainbow rope. A rainbow rope is nothing more than an elastic loop covered in multicolored velour, but in the hands of children it becomes a horse's reins, a fire hose, or the means for many other games. When the children are playing the same game, things go well. They move in the same direction and at the same speed, and their play continues. When, however, each child wants to play a different game, moving in a different direction at a different speed, chaos ensues. Fights break out as the children argue over what to play. If they continue to pull in different directions without intervention, the rope may break, sending kids flying in all directions and causing bruises, tears, and lots of hurt. If the rope does not break, the kids are likely to get bored with going nowhere, give up the rope, and find something else to do.

The same is true of congregations. When dreams, goals, and daily decision making are not in sync, something serious happens to the congregation. No matter what is done or said, it will not measure up to one of these sets of expectations, someone will always be disappointed, and the pastor or ruling board who tries to please people in such a congregation will burn out in exhaustion. That was the situation facing First Church in the annual review. People were not pleased despite extensive planning and multiple efforts. People gave up on the congregation, because all it did was drift. It went nowhere, did nothing important, said nothing significant. Like the children with the rainbow rope, people got bored with the congregation, left it, and found something else to do.

Even so, First Church was lucky. Rainbow ropes can break if pulled in too many directions, and congregations can explode when the tension among differing dreams, goals, and daily life becomes too great to contain. In one congregation I know, the pastor neglected members' dreams for his own. The contrast between his goals and members' dreams created friction that broke out as petty bickering, made members unwilling to help the pastor's family during a major health crisis, and resulted in the pastor being advised to leave in less than two years. In another congregation, unrecognized dreams contributed to the development of factions. When conflict occurred over an unrelated issue, these factions produced rancorous congregational meetings in which groups accused each other of trying to take over by stacking the votes, packing the boards, and excluding others. The accumulated tension exploded, leaving behind misunderstandings, hurt feelings, broken relationships, and a deep sense of betrayal at members' inability to live out their calling as church.

ARTICULATING A NEW VISION

So what do we do? How do we address the dissatisfaction that develops when a congregation's dreams, goals, and daily decision making are so out of sync that members dream of building a cathedral but end up with a skyscraper? The first task is to learn how to uncover members' dreams, and asking does not always do it. Questions have to be properly phrased to uncover the information we are looking for. For example, if we ask about needs, we will find out about needs, but as pointed out above, needs are not the same as dreams. Similarly, people's assumptions influence their answers. If we ask people what they want from a congregation, most will answer with regard to what they assume congregations provide–Bible studies, fellowship, sermons, and music. If these are not what they are looking for, their blunt response may be, "What do I want from the church? Nothing!" All the while their dream of finding an environment that is spiritually nurturing and helps them encounter God goes unexpressed and unaddressed.

The more helpful question to ask people is: How would you shape a congregation if you were starting one from scratch? What kinds of things would you have this congregation do, or avoid doing? Being freed from the politics involved in changing "the way we've always done it" seems to open people to alternatives and thus to dreams. They can talk about other ways of doing things without seeming critical of the past.

Many people have trouble articulating their dreams of what a congregation could be. An additional complication is that many mission assessment procedures provide only two ways of discussing what it means to be the church. They speak of the church either as a servant in the world caring for people's needs or as a herald proclaiming the news of Christ. They overlook other ways of being the church as well as the dreams that fit those other ways.

I have found Avery Dulles's *Models of the Church*[2] helpful in giving people a language with which to articulate their dreams. In small groups, I ask people to discuss the three questions Dulles used to shape his models: What are the bonds that hold us together as church? Who benefits from our existence? What benefits do they receive? After presenting Dulles's models, I ask people to identify where they fit and use their answers to structure a statement about what it means for them to be the church. In the years I have used this exercise, I have found members of most congregations have a remarkably consistent understanding of what it means for their congregation to be church. It may not be the understanding expressed in their mission study. It may not be the understanding discussed in Sunday worship. But there is a consistency among the members.

In recent years I have also found a change in the models that congregation members claim speak to them. When I first used this exercise, people tended to choose the herald or servant models. In the past ten years no congregation has chosen those models. Every congregation has spoken of itself in terms reflective of Dulles's sacramental or mystical communion models. I believe that this change, which is not reflected in the mission assessment procedures I have seen, contributes to the gap that so often develops between dreams, goals, and day-to-day decision making.

Do We Have a Workable Blueprint?

Once the dream is identified, the second task is finding ways to examine whether the parts of a congregation's life are working together. Neither doing a new mission study, writing a new mission statement, developing new programs, nor calling a new pastor will do it alone. These actions may change a congregation's goals or its daily decision making, but they will not address whether the parts are in conflict with one another. This examination involves looking closely at our ideas about building congregations, especially those ideas we accept without question. What kind of congregations do our ideas actually lead us to build, and are these really the kinds of communities we dream of creating?

So how do we look at our ideas? One place to start is with books discussing what it means to be the church. Reading and discussing books such as Leander E. Keck's *The Church Confident* (Abingdon Press, 1993), Charles Van Engen's *God's Missionary People: Rethinking the Purpose of the Local Church* (Baker Book House, 1991), and Russell Chandler's *Racing Toward 2001* (Zondervan Publishing House, 1992) can expand our perception of what the church can be. More important, however, is to translate those new perceptions into action. For that, we need to encourage each other both in ongoing conversations and by sharing ways of taking specific new actions, because it is easy to slip back to doing things "the way we've always done them."

Using Dulles's questions, as described above, to uncover our own understandings of church is an exercise that can be done either individually or in small groups. The surprise is how much change discussions based on these questions can trigger. I have seen congregations change or clarify their ministries in practical ways after a single retreat!

NOTES

1. Kathleen Norris, *Cloister Walk* (New York: Riverhead Books, 1996), p. 65.

2. Avery Dulles, S.J., *Models of the Church* (Garden City, N.Y.: Doubleday & Company, Inc., 1974).

From Congregations: The Alban Journal *14, no. 1 (January/February 1999): pp. 18-21.*

CHAPTER 12

Finding Our Mission

Stages in the Life of an Urban Congregation

Robert T. Roberts

Others have outlined, diagrammed, and described the life cycles of congregations. Others have studied congregations in a variety of stages and settings. What I want to set forth here is more a journal of the stages I have experienced in the life of one struggling congregation where I have served as pastor for 22 years.

Believing that there is no such thing as a typical congregation, I make no claims that what I describe is normative. There is a strong chance, however, that it may be instructive and illustrative of stages other congregations follow. In fact, I am convinced that our passage through these stages has not been the result of any grand strategy of the pastor, the session, and certainly not the presbytery. Rather, as we have sought in some manner to be faithful to the Gospel as we have perceived it and to be open to the leading of the Spirit, we have found ourselves emerging at new places along this journey. In fact, many of our strategies and long-range plans have been counterproductive. This is not to eschew planning and strategizing. Indeed, the more difficult the congregation's setting and context for ministry, the more urgent and compelling is the need to plan, set goals, and define mission. Experience has taught me, however, to remain loosely invested in all projections, schemes, and carefully defined directions.

As we push our way through the thicket, looking for landmarks to guide us, it is at those places where we can more clearly see the lay of the land that we can find new points to aim our efforts.

So now—looking back—the outline of the stages through which we have made our way begins to take shape.

STAGE ONE: AN ESTABLISHED CONGREGATION

The central-city congregation had declining membership and had long since been disestablished when I arrived as the young and promising pastor. For one thing, the old, established, once prestigious neighborhood had long ago fallen into disfavor among the status conscious. Far too many mainline denominational congregations had been planted in this part of the city, leaving them to compete with each other for the dwindling supply of "their kind" of people. The Protestant churches clung tenaciously to members long removed from the neighborhood. However, it was easier to retain these members than to attract newer and more heterogeneous residents. In our case, the congregation had declined from 800 to 250 members. The neighborhood was a low-income port of entry for rural immigrants. The remnant leaders were "drive-in" members. The neighborhood members were mostly older couples or more often single adults "trapped" in the neighborhood by economic realities.

However, the memory of the established congregation still dominated those early years of my pastorate.

STAGE TWO: EFFORTS TO REESTABLISH

Upon my arrival, the dominant theme of the search committee and the congregational leaders was to align the future of the congregation with the neighborhood; however, the unspoken goal was to reestablish the congregation as it had been in the past. Much well meant effort was expended seeking to restore disaffected and inactive members. And when it was blithely stated—as it endlessly was—that our future was with the neighborhood, virtually no one, including the eager young pastor, fully understood what that meant. What was envisioned was that somewhere among these community folk were replacements for the lost members and leaders of the past. When few "genuine factory replacements" were found, an effort was made to fashion substitute spare parts into something as near the originals as possible. Few of us could comprehend that if the future was in the neighborhood, it was the congregation that would need to change.

STAGE THREE: GRIEF

Not long after arriving on the scene, I attended a seminar on grief, which I eagerly perceived as being part of my continuing pastoral education. It almost turned into a career! Listening to the leader describe the early landmark study of grief among the survivors of a disastrous fire in 1944, a strange thought caught my attention. In his psychological study, Eric Lindemann described common physical characteristics of the grieving experience. He then listed a number of characteristic psychological symptoms: preoccupation with the image of the deceased, preoccupation with guilt, tendency toward anger, tendency toward dependency. Suddenly, it seemed to me that in addition to accurately describing individual grief, the seminar leader was painting a rather detailed portrait of the congregation I was serving. This insight led me to complete a doctoral study on this aspect of the life of our congregation and others in decline. The aim of my work was to assist congregations, pastors, and denominational leaders to understand more pastorally this dynamic in congregations that are experiencing loss of self-esteem, at a time when the church still talks as if numerical growth is the normative pattern for all Christendom. Using the now familiar insights of Elisabeth Kubler-Ross and others, I sought to show that much of the puzzling and even frustrating behavior in declining congregations can be understood as grief.

STAGE FOUR: REINVESTMENT

When individuals grieve, a significant part of the process is reinvesting energies and commitments in new directions, activities, and people. The reinvestment is not only a step toward wholeness, but is in fact a sign that grief is being resolved and the past has been released. This is an important time of letting go for both pastor and congregation.

For our congregation, the overwhelming needs of a deteriorating neighborhood helped us move through the grieving process. The opportunities for mission were so compelling that tentatively at first, and then almost recklessly, we began to invest ourselves in new and challenging forms of ministry.

STAGE FIVE: SURVIVAL

Emerging from a prolonged period of grief, our next sticking point was survival. Although we were committed to ministry, we nevertheless made decisions based on a bottom line that the congregation must survive. Painfully aware of diminished resources--money, leadership, and people--programs and projects were adopted based on minimal drain on these resources. Constantly aware of vanishing wealth, there was an effort to collect overflowing baskets of food and mete out only a couple of loaves and a handful of fish. Like the third steward in Jesus's parable, we were painfully aware of having fewer resources than others, which lead us to take minimal risks to ensure the survival of what little we had.

STAGE SIX: MISSION AS DESPERATION

The next three stages, the mission stages, represent a reorientation toward the future. However, each step is distinctive.

Gradually, in our case, in ways and for reasons not yet clear to me, the congregation came unstuck from a survival mentality. Perhaps it was a growing awareness that we had outlived any reasonable expectation of survival as a middle-class congregation in a blue-collar to low-income, ethnically and racially diverse community. Maybe it was a quasi-resurrection experience. Perhaps it was a growing acknowledgment that if God had not intended this congregation exist, it would have been long gone anyway. For whatever reason, we relaxed during this period. We were no longer frantically rowing in all directions at once; there was more willingness to go with the flow and trust the process. Suddenly, there was openness to all mission endeavors.

In this stage, we learned that desperation was a kind of strange ally. Almost anything was worth a try. Creative uses of remaining resources became possible. We tried linking with other congregations. Somehow, anyhow, we would find a way to reach out and bridge the gap between congregation and neighborhood. Risk was no barrier.

STAGE SEVEN: MISSION AS A MEANS TO AN END

Gradually, we moved from tentative efforts to be of service to the neighborhood, to more sophisticated and complex efforts. A housing corporation enabled a $2.33 million apartment development. A Neighborhood House served community youths and adults. A grassroots preschool emerged. A separate corporation for community ministry was developed. Emergency assistance grew. Mental health programs and recreational programs were designed. Community organizational efforts were launched, neighborhood victories were won, and a new sense of belonging emerged in the community. No longer did the congregation wallow in self-pity and self-doubt. Rather self-affirmation grew as we experienced the true miracle of the loaves and fishes. As we poured our limited resources into these efforts with abandonment, we were amazed to see our meager offerings multiplied by other resources that seemed to appear daily from the most unexpected places. The congregation could and did feel gratified at the amazing developments in its community-serving mode.

However, with this apparent success a new bafflement emerged. Hordes of community folk passed through the building for six days a week. But where were these people on Sunday? Why were they not lined up at the doors each Sunday, eager to express their gratitude for all the great things we were doing on their behalf? Mission as a means of returning the congregation to numerical growth and prosperity was not working.

STAGE EIGHT: MISSION AS AN END IN ITSELF

Gradually the awareness began to sink in. Many of the people we saw during the week were church members elsewhere. Their congregations did not provide the programs or services they could find from us, but their spiritual needs were being met elsewhere. Still, a vast gulf separated our congregation's style of worship and the informal, more emotionally engaging styles attractive to most neighborhood folk. An occasional neighborhood person entered the life of the congregation through involvement in our ministries. Usually, the person had already moved from recipient to volunteer or even to staff member, but the ingathering was sparse.

By this time, however, mission and service had become a way of life for our congregation. A few neighborhood folk had joined us, and the lifestyle of the congregation had become more informal, open, flexible, and less threatened by the style and nature of neighborhood people. But the turning point came when the dominant attitude of the congregation moved from commitment to service as a way to attract members, to a commitment to do ministry as the nature of Christian discipleship, even if no community person ever crossed the threshold on a Sunday. Strangely, when that mood of ministry for its own sake took over, neighborhood folk began moving into the life of the congregation in significant numbers.

STAGE NINE: SPIRITUAL NURTURE

A new awareness makes its way into the congregation's priorities. Mission and service are givens. The need alone requires it. And the congregation's understanding of its own need to reach out mandates it. But clearly, outreach as a singular focus is not enough. Like breathing out without breathing in, it just will not work. Increasingly, the congregation finds itself at this point intent on strengthening the quality of its own worship and spiritual nurture. Only a rich worship life can sustain a vibrant ministry of service. Outreach ministry is not in question. It is a given. Congregational diversity has also become a way of life. Awareness that we do not live in isolation, but exist in partnership, is a constant part of our contextual landscape. In our own community, as part of an urban network and globally, we worship and minister in relationship. But central to this stage is the issue of the quality of the worship, nurture, and spiritual life of the congregation. Members are eager to attract others into the life of this particular faith community, not only because of a commitment to mission, but also for the quality of its internal life. Clearly in this stage the congregation has returned to affirmation of itself, but affirmation in a context of mission.

THE JOURNEY CONTINUES

The account of this journey is intended to be descriptive rather than prescriptive. It is more anecdotal than scientific. Much of our pilgrimage is no doubt typical and reflects the experience of similar congregations in similar settings. Some may trace these steps almost identically. Others may take side journeys, add stages, or get stuck at one place or another. Those in the earlier stages of grief or survival may take heart that exciting days may well lie ahead. Others may have moved beyond our place and hold in their story promise for us. We strain forward with eagerness toward whatever new styles and stages await our continued journey.

It is my conviction that urban congregations need to share with each other their stories and their process. We need to testify to each other what we have learned of both the terrifying obstacles and the rich rewards that may lie ahead. We need each other's reports and testimonies as we live our ways through the wilderness.

Rich diversity is one of the delightful surprises of urban congregations. However, I am convinced there is much in our unfinished story that will ring true for other congregations who like us are pilgrims in the city. We need each other as we learn to live in the city, embrace the city, confront the city, and act as heralds of the kingdom in the city.

From Action Information *14, no. 5 (September/October 1998): pp. 12-14.*

CHAPTER 13

Congregations in Decline

How Context Affects Size

Alice Mann

L ots of churches are grappling with decline and do not know what to do about it. From World War II until about 1965, congregations overall saw membership grow rapidly. From 1965 until rather recently, though, the total membership of mainline congregations has declined significantly, while the population of the United States has increased. Most congregations do not realize the degree to which their community context drives congregational growth and decline trends.

When congregations notice a decrease in Sunday school attendance or worship attendance, or feel a financial crunch, they tend to attribute that change to internal factors. The most popular ones: If we are declining, there must be something wrong with our pastor. Or, our board is doing something wrong. Or, we ought to go back to that successful program we had in 1955.

ALthough it is true that pastoral leadership, the leadership of the board, and church programs are important, what most congregations miss is the fundamental connection between faith and context. The problem comes when the environment around the church changes. In a sense, faith communities are inherently conserving; they are carriers of traditions. There is great staying power in the community's deep connection with tradition. But there is also great danger for congregations in the natural hesitance to reinterpret that tradition for a new context.

COMMON MISTAKES

One mistake congregations make when they begin to decline is that they refuse to look at the trends and the facts. Frequently congregations stop keeping accurate records, or if they do keep records, they do not organize them, share them, graph them—really keep track of what is happening. They avoid paying attention to what might be bad news.

The second is that as soon as that information comes out, their first response is to blame, and the candidate for blame is frequently the pastor. The tendency is to look internally and say, "If only we had a new pastor. If only the denomination were still sending us that great curriculum. If only we did not have controversy about difficult issues." This blame breeds defensiveness, which escalates conflic, and unmanaged conflict distracts attention from the fundamental work of reconnecting faith and context.

The third mistake is that typically, when a church first starts to officially notice a problem, there is a tendency to grab an answer, often a programmatic answer, before the problem is understood. If the congregation does not back up and take a long view—30 years—at the trends, it is likely to put a lot of resources into an answer that is probably too small. When that answer does not work, frustration and despair rise even higher, and the blame becomes even more intense.

That is how congregations get into declining spirals. They just do not look broadly enough at what is creating the crunch, so they act in ways that reinforce the spiral. But some congregations look at the bigger picture and figure out approaches that could mitigate the spiral. They launch a new era of growth out of that experience. Congregations need to ask, What choices do we have about how we respond to the changes we are experiencing?

CHALLENGES FOR DECLINING CONGREGATIONS

The greatest challenge to declining congregations is to face the possibility that the congregation's work is finished. That might sound like despair, but it is the beginning of letting go of survival as the chief motivation. Congregations need to ask, What was the work God assigned us in the beginning, and is that work finished? If a congregation has the courage to look at that question—which means facing the possibility of its own death—it has also opened itself to the possibility of framing a fresh mission based on its historic values.

That is a thrilling moment for me. There is something so fundamentally faithful about it. It is a moment full of spiritual meaning for the people who participate in it, and they know they have accomplished some great work for God when they have struggled down to that question of vocation and have begun to see the glimmer of a new direction.

HOPE IN THE FACE OF CHALLENGE

In a way, I judge my work as a church consultant by the number of faith communities that are able to engage the vocation question in a variety of ways: How did we bring faith to context in our founding? How was God at work in the energies that gave rise to this congregation at its beginnings? How is God at work today? What is our call in this moment, in this context? When congregations have engaged those questions deeply and honestly, I always find energy for significant ministry, even if that ministry involves dying and transferring resources.

I am always afraid to talk about the dying part, for fear of being misinterpreted. I have never advocated quickly closing struggling congregations. I deeply believe that within any denominational strategy in a particular region, there needs to be a very vigorous balance between starting new congregations and helping existing congregations to reframe the relationship between faith and context. Those two ministries feed each other. The new starts draw energy from the big trends in the environment and provide momentum and hopefulness for a given moment. The redevelopment work provides assurance that transformation is possible.

Every new start is eventually going to encounter some major change in its context that threatens its existence. That is inevitable, especially given the pace of change in our communities. Redeveloping congregations have something to teach the whole church about facing facts courageously, relinquishing blame, and finding the presence of God in change, in challenge, even in failure.

Adapted from an interview in Congregations: The Alban Journal *16, no. 3 (May/ June 2000): pp. 22-23.*

CHAPTER 14

When Membership Declines

Letting Go and Moving Forward

Roy M. Oswald

There are times when, no matter how capable, clergy cannot reverse the downward slide of congregational membership. The reasons may be simply demographic: at times certain areas of the country become depressed and begin to decline in population. In these areas, the older people may stay, but younger people need to move elsewhere to find work.

What are the parish dynamics when a congregation becomes smaller? What do clergy moving into those congregations need to pay attention to when the membership shrinks to the next size?

From Corporate- to Program-Size Church

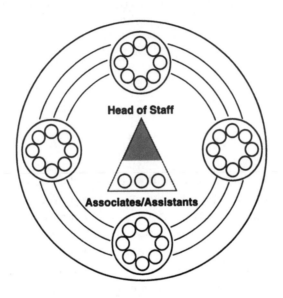

The first thing these congregations are likely to lose is their ability to support a large multiple staff. The decision to cut down the full- and part-time church staff requires care. Areas of ministry that have been managed by the core staff will need to be turned over to church volunteers. All corporate-size churches depend upon volunteers to do much of the work. Lay leaders who chair important committees have had the benefit of a staff person to confer with and to manage some of the administrative work of the committees. When staff is cut, these lay volunteers will need to take charge more fully, delegating the follow-through work that was previously carried out by a staff person.

Corporate-size churches often have amassed some endowment funds. There will be a strong temptation to use some of these funds to support certain staff positions with the rationale that these staff members will help the church regain its former size. Such a strategy needs to be evaluated carefully. It may set up the staff members for failure, because the church lacks the commitment, energy, and potential to make these former ministries flourish. Instead, new areas of ministry, which do have vision and commitment behind them, may need to be developed. If so, they will discover their own funding and not be dependent upon endowment funds.

Deciding which staff positions to cut is difficult work, yet it must be done. It is easy to get caught between loyalties to faithful, hardworking staff members and a mission emphasis that might dictate retaining areas of ministry that do not correspond to these staff member's skills.

The place to start with all these decisions is to engage the leaders of the parish in an assessment and planning process. I would recommend engaging an outside consultant and allowing plenty of time for this period of reflection, letting go, assessment, and goal setting. I recommend beginning with a historical reflection process in which members can review the history of the parish, identify the strengths that have characterized the church's past and that need to be built into its future. Leaders can then confront directly some of the reasons for the decline in membership. Important grieving needs to take place during this process. To move too quickly to a mission statement would be to short-circuit an important developmental stage in moving to a new identity as a program-size church. People are going to have to let go of an image and an identity of being the biggest and the best. The program-size church has many strengths, yet the core leaders may not see those strengths because they have not adequately dealt with their grief about the death of their churches former image.

FROM PROGRAM- TO PASTORAL-SIZE CHURCH

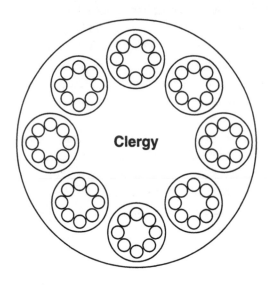

Just as the movement from pastoral- to program-size church is experienced as the most difficult and traumatic, so moving from program- to pastoral-size church will present the congregation with a difficult transition. An identity needs to be relinquished. The wonderful team of volunteers that made everything happen in the church has largely disappeared. Many probably left because of burnout and sought a corporate-size church where they could rest and have their wounds healed.

There may be a faithful core remaining who will be tempted to try to pump up the church again by sheer commitment and energy. This faithful remnant needs to be spared the discouragement inherent in such an effort. Some serious downsizing needs to take place whereby all the separate program emphases of the parish are collapsed into a few small working groups. For example, rather than having separate committees for evangelism, stewardship, Christian education, property, social ministry, music, and worship, these all may need to be combined into a committee on parish life or to be reclaimed by the vestry/session/council/consistory. One person on these decision-making groups can receive all the mail from the national church on one particular program emphasis. That person will occasionally head up a task force to accomplish certain goals in that area of ministry when such an effort is deemed important by the chief decision-making body.

The key issue in downsizing from program to pastoral size is the responsible management of volunteer energies. A program-size church that shrinks to pastoral size will surely burn out its lay leaders. Soon cynicism, disillusionment, and fatigue begin to permeate the whole parish. People start serving on two or three committees just to keep them afloat. It is difficult to get the committees to do anything significant, because everyone is simply too tired.

The downsizing strategy may include suspending all parish committees and programs and declaring sabbaticals for all parish leaders. During this time the parish should focus on activities that spiritually nurture the parish leaders. The sabbatical period should end with a retreat or workshop at which members are invited to assess where God seems to be calling them to serve.

During or following this period of suspended activity, key leaders can be invited to an assessment and planning process. What parish identity is both viable and energy-generating? Once members have gone through the process of grieving the loss of their former identity, they can discern a vision of the pastoral-size church that fills them with hope and excitement. Can this group once again find energy in doing things as a single unit, such as having parish dinners and activities in which everyone can participate? As they move from multiple services to one worship service, can they begin to feel the advantages of having everyone worshipping together again?

Finally, can they begin to appreciate having more quality time with their pastor? Can they begin to allow their pastor to become the primary source of their spiritual feeding? What was done formerly in formal program settings can now be done informally around the edges. The pastor can again know my teenage son personally rather than having to ensure that there is a youth group to minister to him. The pastor needs to let go of many administrative and program developmental tasks and begin to appear in people's lives in a variety of informal settings. Visiting people in their places of employment to experience the context of a person's ministry there might be a good place to start. People will let go of some of their program needs much more easily when they begin to feel more cared for personally.

From Pastoral- to Family-Size Church

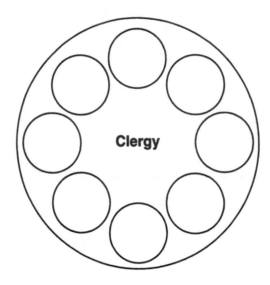

This transition will be inaugurated by a congregation's discovery that it can no longer support a full-time ordained person. This is likely to occur when a pastor resigns, and in working things through with their middle judicatory officials, the church leaders become clear that they can no longer afford a pay package that will meet the minimum salary scale set by the denomination.

This discovery is often a traumatic point in the life of a parish. Members see inability to afford their own pastor as a sign of failure. For many of the older members, the loss is seen in no longer having a pastor to live in their parsonage. We should not underestimate the unconscious anxiety that is produced in the lives of many people when they realize they do not have a religious authority available to them around the clock. They may rarely have taken advantage of the opportunity to call on the services of the person living in their parsonage, yet it was more the possibility than the actuality that was important to them.

One of the clear advantages of a congregation moving from pastoral to family size is that an abnormally high percentage of their income no longer needs to go into supporting a pastor. They may find they have some money to support other kinds of parish activities.

The other advantage, which may come as a blessing in disguise, is that members will need to get clear about what pastoral services are essential in order for them to function well as a religious community. That clarity has the effect of helping the parish leaders become clear about the roles and responsibilities that will not be covered by a pastor and that need to be picked up by lay volunteers. Seen in a positive light, this clarity can open up opportunities for fulfilling ministries for some lay leaders.

True to its nature as a patriarchal/matriarchal church, the parish needs to assume control of its own life, taking over all leadership functions and delegating pastoral care ministries to clergy. The members need to stay focused on the direction of their parish and not allow it to be swayed by the ideas of clergy who have only a temporary investment in the parish.

FROM FAMILY-SIZE CHURCH TO NONEXISTENCE

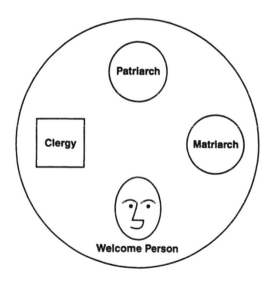

There have been congregations that, when confronted with the alternative of either living or dying, have made the conscious decision to die. In the process of dying well, they generated so much energy that they changed their minds. One United Church of Christ congregation in St. Louis hired an interim pastor who was to help them die well. Eight years later they had become a thriving congregation.

A Christian Church (Disciples of Christ) congregation in Bethesda, Maryland, voted two years ago to terminate their life, and they have effectively done so, merging their assets with a neighboring congregation. Their long-term pastor saw them through the closure and was himself awarded a sabbatical once the parish had closed. Their decision was quite deliberate, and even though they had endowment funds that could have kept them open, they choose instead to end with dignity and merge with a neighboring congregation.

The above two examples are anecdotal. I suspect there are more such examples of churches dealing effectively with decline. It would be helpful if churches could chose from a variety of models for decline, so they could get better at shutting down more quickly and effectively. In this era of church decline, some congregations need and want to die, but dying well is qualitatively different from simply fading into oblivion. We need to learn how to help churches die well.

From Action Information *17, no. 3 (May/June 1991): pp. 5-7.*

CHAPTER 15

The Death and Dying
of a Congregation

An Experience of God's Grace

Daphne Burt

Ministering to a congregation that is dying is a special challenge to a parish pastor. Just as doctors are trained to fight off disease and promote wellness, so are pastors taught to open and nurture churches, not close them. In a dying parish, the pastor encounters some of the same reactions and responses as when ministering to a terminally ill patient. The people of the parish see themselves as one body that they have birthed, sustained, and supported. As a corporate unity, the parishioners resist the church's death. For many, the fact that the church is dying means that a part of them is dying as well.

Elisabeth Kubler-Ross delineated five distinct stages through which a dying person passes.[1] They are not always experienced one after another; sometimes they overlap. Those stages—denial, anger, bargaining, depression, and acceptance—are all experienced by the members of a dying church. What follows is an analysis of how the parish served by the author passed through all five. Not all parishes that close will have the same dynamics—the age, structure, and history of each congregation will clearly have a bearing on the reaction to closing. (As an example, one pastor who closed a parish noted that the existence of a parish-owned cemetery added complications to the grief process.) It is hoped that the discussion of how one parish went through this often painful process may prove helpful to those pastors who find themselves confronted by this ministry situation.

DENIAL

Denial was probably the most powerful dynamic in the dying parish the author served. One of the reasons that this parish had survived as long as it had was the tenacity and faithfulness of members who refused to give up. Therefore, one of the most difficult obstacles the pastor had to deal with was rampant denial. The same people who would admit in private that it would be better if the church would close, would sit at a council meeting and say to everyone, "Let's give it one more chance." The treasurer, mutual ministry committee chairperson, and pastor would report month after month that attendance, giving, and support were not adequate for the parish to maintain itself. The council appeared not to have heard the message. Members seemed to be harboring the fantasy that "all they needed was for God to send a busload of people looking for a Lutheran church," as the frustrated council vice president put it. Members of the Bible study group chose to study a curriculum that emphasized ways to affect church growth.

Ministering to parishioners whose mood would swing from open-eyed acceptance of the reality to close-minded denial proved to be difficult and frustrating. The pastor felt compelled to speak firmly but gently about the reality that the current situation was not temporary, but terminal, and that the appropriate action was to take the steps necessary to go about disbanding the parish. However, the pastor also had to keep in mind that ultimately it was not up to her to decide to close the parish; that decision needed to be made by the congregation. The necessity to speak the truth, yet remain open to the doubts, fears, and denial of parishioners, required a great deal of sensitivity and patience. This was not always possible. During this time the pastor realized the need for a strong support system outside the parish in order to keep some perspective and deal positively with the denial she encountered.

ANGER

Even as it is considered by many to be taboo to express anger about death and dying, so also was it difficult for parishioners to express their anger about the closing of their parish. Often their anger went underground and was expressed passive-aggressively. Members began to avoid one another because they felt the others to be at fault. Much time was spent in the search for a scapegoat on which to dump all the blame and anger. At various times, the scapegoat was the previous pastor(s), the deployed staff of the Division for Mission, the industry that had closed its local plant, or the members of the parish who had "jumped ship" while the parish was still floundering. The members who had stopped coming to worship, feeling that they had done all that they could and did not want to have anything further to do with the parish, were of special concern to the pastor. Many of these people were extremely angry and refused to consider membership at any church. However, the pressing needs of active members ultimately took priority over the needs of those who were inactive.

Even as family members quarrel, using laundry lists of sins to throw back and forth at one another, so also did church members in this stage tend to review the mistakes that others had made. Memories were quite vivid, because this was a relatively young parish (less than thirty years old). Many of the last remnant of active members were charter members who could recall the entire history of the congregation.

The pastor was challenged to enable members to express their anger rather than swallow it, and to separate the fables and family lore from the truth. When parishioners perceived that the pastor could not handle their anger, which was sometimes the case, they would refrain from expressing it. This meant that their anger was allowed to fester and become more powerful.

Some members were able to admit being angry with God. "Why has God deserted us?" "Why did God bring us to this point and let us flounder?" "Where is God when we need strength and support?" were questions typically asked by parishioners. The pastor could not answer, only listen.

BARGAINING

As a dying patient bargains with God in the hope of finding a way out of the inevitable, so the parishioners of the dying parish bargained with God. The closer the moment of closure came, the more frantic the bargaining became.

Parishioners' views of the role God played in the closure of the parish surfaced in most stages of dying but were most clearly evidenced in the bargaining stage. It appeared that, whether articulated or not, members wanted to try to influence God by starting last-minute programs (such as the Bible study on evangelism) with the hope that God would be pleased and the future of the parish would once again be secure. "All we need is to have one family join and four inactives return, and then God will know we're doing our job" was a typical opening to such a discussion. Bargaining became a kind of "works righteousness" game, normally abhorrent to Lutherans and impossible to win. The complement to "if we do the right thing then God will 'reward us'" is "since God is punishing us, we must have done something wrong, and if we can figure out what it is and change it, God will stop." The pastor was called upon to interpret what God's will might be for the parish. This was often as elusive for the pastor as for the members, but the pastor was able to suggest with candor that it might indeed be God's will that the parish close. This was a liberating message to some members, allowing them to be freed from the deadly cycle of bargaining with God. These members could then turn their energies toward accepting the reality and going about the business of closing the parish.

DEPRESSION

Like a funeral pall over the denial, anger, and bargaining, an overwhelming feeling of depression shrouded many parishioners' lives. Unable to accept the fact that the congregation was dying, the members became increasingly depressed, as though they were one body. Time dragged endlessly on. Members began to show signs of listlessness, loss of sleep, and lack of interest. They began to lose all affect, positive and negative. They were apt to berate themselves with "it's my fault" language. In their struggle to keep their spirits up, parishioners often turned again to denying the problem and refusing to acknowledge that they were depressed. These feelings presented the pastor with an uncomfortable dynamic during home visitation. On one hand, members wanted and needed to be visited, so that they could express those feelings that they were still not ready for other members to hear. On the other hand, a visit from the pastor meant that members were going to be reminded of the reality they did not want to face, even if the pastor did not bring it up. The pastor was challenged to be sensitive to those feelings and to be aware of the need to leave people alone from time to time.

ACCEPTANCE

Just as the acceptance of death's inevitability can allow a patient to attend to whatever last things need to be done, so also the acceptance of the fact that the parish would close released the energies of the parishioners. Instead of pouring tremendous amounts of effort into saving the parish, members who accepted the reality of closure began to be able to pay attention to the well-being of other members. Because not everyone came to acceptance at the same time, those who had arrived at this stage could comfort the depressed and provide reality therapy for those who were still trying to bargain with God.

A certain amount of acceptance was necessary before the church council could call a special meeting of the congregation to vote on disbanding. Council members had to move past their own denial in order to do this. The sticking point seemed to be that no one wanted to be the only one who was ready for the church to close. It became difficult for those who had accepted the inevitable to express their feelings, because they feared they would be labeled as traitors or would make the other members angry. Once it was clear that many members accepted the need for closure, the pastor could provide a safe setting for members to share their feelings with one another.

Acceptance of the reality enabled parishioners to put their energies into a meaningful and therapeutic closing. Following the congregational vote, members set about tasks of inventorying church property, planning the final worship, and beginning to look to the future. There were many tears shed and many hugs given during this time. Caught between memories of the past and promises of the future, parishioners were able to begin to share with one another their deepest feelings. Such moments were more than cathartic, for by remembering the past and discussing the future, the health and attitudes of the members improved. Members felt closer to each other, which helped them to share their grief.

Parishioners were encouraged to look at their future any way that they could. Visiting other parishes' worship services was encouraged, so that members could decide where they wanted their new church home to be. One family made that decision and arranged for their membership to be transferred the day after the parish closed. Another member expressed her joy in remembering by preparing a bulletin board filled with photographs and clippings that illustrated the parish history. As more space and time was provided for the sharing of stories, the more healing of memories occurred, and acceptance of the parish death became more complete.

DEATH

On Sundays following the congregational vote, the preaching focused on the proclamation of the resurrection. This pastor found the metaphor of a "garden of God" to be helpful, speaking of the parishioners as beautiful flowers in God's garden, raised and nurtured to be transplanted into other parishes' gardens, bringing with them their colorful gifts and talents. Although this was certainly a most difficult time for all, it was also a time for much healing. Time was taken to plan a final worship service that was inclusive and that brought the community together to remember and rejoice in the life of witness and service that had been characteristic of the parish.

The date for the closing worship service was set according to the readiness of the parishioners to accept the finality of death, a luxury that most individuals do not have. Although some members were still not ready for the church to disband, others were moved and comforted by the worship service. By having walked through their reactions and feelings about the death of the parish, most were prepared to hear the good news in the promise of resurrection.

CONCLUSION

The dynamics of a dying parish resemble those of a terminally ill person. In order to minister effectively to such a parish, it is helpful to examine the distinct and inevitable stages such a parish might go through, especially as they are similar to those of a dying person. If the pastor can guide the parish through the denial and anger, bargaining and depression, the acceptance of the need to disband can occur. Acceptance then liberates the members to celebrate the life of the parish and to prepare for active membership in a new church home. Ministry to a dying parish can be a rich and awe-filled experience of the mystery of God's activity in the world. To Christians who believe that God transforms death into new and everlasting life, the death of a parish can be a profound and powerful experience of God's grace and love.

NOTE

    1.   Elisabeth Kubler-Ross, *On Death and Dying* (New York: Macmillan Publishing Co., Inc., 1969).

From Action Information *16, no. 4 (July/August 1990): pp. 11-13.*

Daphne Burt is an ordained Lutheran (ELCA) pastor and the associate dean of Rockefeller Chapel at the University of Chicago. Her first call was to Christ Lutheran Church in Bristol, Tennessee. Currently a candidate for a doctor of ministry from the Lutheran School of Theology at Chicago, her current research interests center around issues of sexuality and preaching.

G. Wooden (Woody) Garvin has recently been called to First Presbyterian Church, a vital congregation of 2000 serving the city of Spokane, Washington. He received his master of divinity and doctor of ministry degrees in the area of church growth from San Francisco Theological Seminary. Garvin currently serves on the board of trustees of San Francisco Theological Seminary and Whitworth College.

Dan Hotchkiss is an Alban Institute field consultant based in Boston, Massachusetts. He writes and consults on congregational conflict and planning, clergy leadership, and the interaction of money and faith.

Theodore W. Johnson is an Episcopal priest who has specialized in developmental transitions in congregations. He currently serves a congregation in Southern Maryland. In addition, he is a consultant and leadership developer for congregations in transition. While completing his doctor of ministry degree in congregational development at Seabury-Western Theological Seminary, he worked closely with Arlin J. Rothauge. He lives in Alexandria, Virginia.

Bill Joiner is a Kansas City-based management consultant in private practice. He is also an American Baptist pastor and a former member of the Alban consultant network.

Edward H. Koster is an attorney and Presbyterian minister in Ann Arbor, Michigan, and is the stated clerk of the presbytery of Detroit.

Alice Mann is an Alban Institute senior consultant and author of several books including *The In-Between Church: Navigating Size Transitions in Congregations* and *Can Our Church Live? Redeveloping Congregations in Decline*. She has recently completed a research project on the pastoral- to program-size transition and launched the pilot version of an online course on that topic.

Joel S. McCoy has been pastor of First Baptist Church in Sweetwater, Texas, for almost seven years and has served two other Texas Baptist churches in his twenty years of pastoral ministry. He received his doctor of ministry degree from Southwestern Baptist Theological Seminary in 1989.

Roy M. Oswald is a senior consultant with the Alban Institute. He is the author of numerous Alban publications including *Transforming Rituals: Daily Practices for Changing Lives* and *Discerning Your Congregation's Future: A Strategic and Spiritual Approach* (with Robert E. Friedrich, Jr.).

Ronald T. Roberts is a pastor living in Lake Ozark, Missouri. When the article was written he was the pastor of two congregations, one Presbyterian and one Methodist, in the Kansas City area.

Elizabeth I. Steele lives in Santa Monica, California, where she describes herself as "an unintentional professional interim." She has spent more than twenty years helping congregations in crisis redefine themselves and their ministry.

David Trietsch is director of the Jewish Resource Network Initiative (JRNI), which is under the auspices of Boston's Commission on Jewish Continuity, a partnership between the Combined Jewish Philanthropies and the Union of America Hebrew Congregations, the United Synagogue of Conservative Judaism, Council of Orthodox Synagogues, and Synagogue Council of Massachusetts.

Douglas Alan Walrath of Bangor Theological Seminary is a congregational consultant, expert on the effect of demographic changes on church development, author and editor of several books on church size and transition, and a former Reformed Church in America executive.

LaVergne, TN USA
11 August 2010
192939LV00003B/1/P